MIGRATION TRENDS AND POPULATION CHANGES IN JAMMU AND KASHMIR STATE

MIGRATION TRENDS AND POPULATION CHANGES IN JAMMU AND KASHMIR STATE

B.A. Dabla

KALPAZ

ISBN : 978-93-5128-007-1
Price : ₹ 715

First Published 2014

Published by

Kalpaz Publications
C-30, Satyawati Nagar,
Delhi-110052
Ph. : 9212142040
E-mail: kalpaz@hotmail.com

Laser Typesetting : Deepak Shukla, Delhi
Printed at : Chawala Offset Printers, Delhi

Cataloging in Publication Data--DK
Courtesy: D.K. Agencies (P) Ltd. <docinfo@dkagencies.com>

Dabla, Bashir A.
Migration trends and population changes in Jammu and Kashmir State / B.A. Dabla.
p. cm.
Includes bibliographical references (p.) and index.
ISBN 9789351280071

1. Jammu and Kashmir (India)–Emigration and immigration. 2. Jammu and Kashmir (India)–Population. 3. Jammu and Kashmir (India)–Population–Social aspects. I. Title.

DDC 304.809546 23

Contents

SECTION C: SOCIOLOGICAL IMPLICATIONS OF DEMOGRAPHIC TRANSFORMATION IN J&K

Foreword

Demography studies the phenomenon related directly to the study of human population and its dynamics in terms of factors such as births, deaths, marriages and migration. At the same time, the sub-discipline of 'social demography' deal with the study of sociological dimensions of demographic phenomena connected with fertility, mortality, pattern of population growth, various sociological compositions and consequent population changes. In this thematic context, migration trends and population changes emerge as two Basic and important features of the existing demographic reality which is always prone to change [in size, structure and composition] due to intrinsic dynamic character.

The migration of any type stands as a crucial feature of human society. All countries and civilisations have experienced the movement of their founders and leaders from one place to another place. This process of movement was of voluntaristic as well as involuntaristic nature which depends upon the nature, role, objective and push-pull factoRs It has been observed globally and historically that migration always, triggered through social, economic, political, cultural, religious, and racial factors, has initiated broader process of social transformation among the concerned individuals and groups and later on cultures and civilisations. This situation has emerged as a social-demographic reality in the universal human society irrespective of its differences in race, religion, culture, economy, polity, social structure, education, language and ethnicity.

On the other hand, population changes stand as the fundamental process in human society, especially those related to births, deaths and marriages. In actuality, these processes increased or decreased the number of people, leading to broader transformation at micro-level as well as at macro-level. In addition to normal births and deaths, it also focuses on the impact of events like epidemic, floods, fires, and other human and material disasters Normal rates of births and deaths are analysed critically and explained in terms of their relationship with other sociological variables. In this way, population changes and their input-output processes have remained the subject-matter of studies carried out by sociologists and social demographers.

These demographic and social changes have entered in to a relationship between the two phenomena. While demographic change initiates and encourages social change, the opposite also happens in the same way. In most of the societies, these changes have occurred in cooperation, consonance and with mutual stimulation. This type of socio-demographic transformation has been experienced at the global and regional levels. In reality, all developed and developing societies in the world have undergone such a radical transformation, though in varying degrees.

Like many other societies, the society in the state of J&K has undergone such a kind of transformation in the post-independence period. The state has behaved like other states in India. There may be similarities as well as dissimilarities in the patterns of socio-demographic change. I believe that this pattern falls within the broader pan-Indian framework. As the author of this book has mentioned in several papers, this socio-demographic transformation in J&K has closely followed the all-India pattern.

The author, Dr. B.A. Dabla, my student, friend and colleague, is a serious observer of the changing social situation in his state of domicile, i.e., J&K. He has worked on research papers/studies included in this book for the last nine years The academic quality and standard is certainly appreciable as the author has based all his major propositions on primary sources, particularly census records and other official documents. In all papers, which have been written at different times, the presentation and analysis stand highly objective, comprehensive and scientific and new facts are brought to the fore. Every paper/study stands for a different theme and has got contextual scientific framework and relevant methodology. Specific mention may be made about the empirical studies, which the author has carried out [with his team of research investigators] stand as distinct pieces of research involving very hard intensive labour and enough time.

The overall contribution of this book will be significant. Not much research on the specific topics of this book has been carried out so far inside or outside

J&K. So, this book may be considered as the pioneering academic work which will serve the cause of scholars, students and common readers in the fields of sociology and demography.

Since the author is busy in carrying out serious research focused on the Kashmiri society, I wish that he produces many such publications in future.

Professor Ehsanul Haq

Centre for Studies on Social Systems

School of Social Sciences

New Delhi

Preface

(i) At the all India level, two variables of migration trends and population changes have emerged as dominant and determining variables in the broader process of demographic transformation. Subsequently, these demographic changes provided an environment in which largescale and deeper social transformation was experienced more or less in all states of the country. The wholistic scene of change, progress and development has revealed that both these processes of demographic and social transformation have increased as well as intensified and triggered other charges in other fields of life. This change at the macro level seems symptomatic and representative.

(ii) Like other states in the union of India, the Jammu and Kashmir [J&K] state has also experienced these two micro-level and two macro-level processes of transformation. While the basic processes of migration trends and population changes provided the infrastructural base, the two super-structural processes of demographic and social transformations emerged as the prominent manifestations of this type of change. In the context of the state, this broader, deeper and multi-dimensional processes were increased and intensified on an unprecedented scale. The natural situational factors helped these processes to grow without any break, while the official and unofficial efforts led to newly-created demographic and social situation.

(iii) This book essentially deals with these demographic and social dimensions in the larger dynamics of societal transformation from one particular stage [having one set of characteristics] to other particular stage [having another set of features] in the J&K state in the period after 1947. This work has been carried out within the scientific orientation and sociological framework. The book divides the entire theme in three particular sections, A, B and C as follows:

   (a) Trends of Migration

   (b) Patterns of Population Change

   (c) Sociological Implications of Demographic change

(iv) The section A deals with all major and minor trends of migration which started with solid repercussions for the social order. These trends include the migration trends in the historical past and particularly after 1947 when the feudal political order got demolished and was replaced by the democratic form. Many micro-level migration trends mainly related to Kashmiri handicrafts and skilled and semiskilled workers-artisa have also been analysed. Finally, in the recent past, two major trends of migration have been studied rigorously. These two trends can be identified as "Pandit migration in 1990-1991" and "labour migration from 1970s". Both these processes of out and in migration trends effected the Kashmiri society seriously and radically. So, we tried to know the crucial implications of these trends.

(v) The section B deals with the pattern/s of population changes as was revealed in the census reports repeatedly from 1951 onwards. These changes reflected in the total numbers,proportions/percentages, male-female, rural urban composition, married-unmarried composition, age, income and literacy status. In this section, we based our arguments on the most authentic official source, i.e., census records from 1941 to 2011 and explained the changes according to details inferred from different decadal census records. We specifically concentrated on the census records of 1991, 2001 and 2011.

(vi) The section C in this book deals with the broader sociological implications of these crucial and basic changes mentioned in Sections A and B. These important implications have been identified and analysed empirically in four particular social areas which are:

(a) Impact of late marriages in Kashmir

(b) Impact of increasing suicides

(c) impact of expanding disability

(d) Impact of Pandit migration of 1990-1991

(e) Impact of Labour migration.

There are other chapters of 'Introduction' and 'Conclusion' in the book besides 'selected bibliography'.

(vii) All these studies and research papers in the book have covered the broader universe of J&K state. But, this universe is the province of Kashmir in the cases of above mentioned empirical studies. In this way, the major focuss of these studies has remained the Kashmir unit.

Bashir A. Dabla

Acknowledgements

I feel highly thankful to all those who helped in the fieldwork of empirical studies and in writing research papers included in this book on social demography. Special mention may be made about the fieldwork for the study on late marriage carried out by the M.A. students of the batch of 2009-2010 of the Department of Sociology, University of Kashmir, Srinagar.

Moreover, I will remember the burnt of this academic work at the final stage by my family members at home during extreme cold months of December 2012 to February 2013.

Srinagar, J&K. **B.A. Dabla**

March 2013

1

Introduction: Demogrphic and Social Transformation in J&K

1. Demography

(i) Demography refers essentially to "scientific study of human populations, primarily with respect to their size, their structure and their development." It is also generally used to denote the study of phenomena connected directly with human populations such as births, deaths, marriages, migration and so on. It also includes the study of related factors in societies in which fertility rates are being brought under rational human control and attached with economic, social and psychological factoRs It has been observed that demographers have taken active interest in the past in these areas and have explained the "actual reproductive performance" which stood different from physiological capacity to reproduce called 'fecundity'. Thus the study of fertility patterns and trends imply that demographers are really interested in social control of reproduction, and in the study of marriage patterns, it is particularly in this field that demographers make contact with other social sciences such as sociology, economics and social psychology. They have shown increasing interest in the study of attitudes and motivations related to childbearing and childrearing in order to explain variations between different societies or within the same society over different periods. Sometimes, these academic themes are collectively used as population studies. Another aspect of demography deals with academic efforts to forecast future population movements or trends or projections. These arithmetical techniques used in forecasting were relatively simple and routine at the earlier stage but have become complex in introducing computers in this field.

Thus demography today includes a study of the statistical techniques and relations existing within a population as well as of the historical and social factors influencing population movements.

2. Social Demography

(i) It stood for a subject which dealt with the sociological dimensions of demographic phenomena, especially demographic processes related to fertility, mortality, growth, their different social compositions and the consequent demographic transformation. It also emphasised the study of social dynamics of population in terms of its social causation, social implications and establishing co-relation between these phenomena. In this theoretical-thematic context, particular processes of migration trends and population changes have emerged as two core, crucial and dominant themes in the field of social demography.

3. Trends of Migration

(i) Migration refers to the movement of members of society from one place of residence /origin/stay to other place of residence/origin/stay temporarily or permanently. This has been explained in detail in chapter 2. This process has necessarily certain social causes and, at the same time, social implications. That is why the sociologists have concentrated on the study of varying trends of migration as one of the significant subject-matter in their discipline. In this background, the sociologists have studied and focused on the nature, types, patterns, context, contents, and implications of this demographic and social transformation.

(ii) As has been explaind, migration has been experienced at the global-international, regional and national-local levels and people undertook movement at all these levels which had definite causes and consequences. At the global level, it has happened:

- From one continent to another continent/s
- From one sub-continent to other sub-continent
- From one region to other region/s
- From one country to other country/ies
- From many countries to other many countries.

(iii) This global-international migration of sociological type which was carried out in the second half of twentieth century has been identified and explained by Robin Cohin and Paul Kennedy and these trends are mentioned as below:

(a) ***Growth of refugee migration:*** General estimates revealed that current number of refugees at the global level is between 18 to 20 million people, which include children, women and elderly.

(b) ***Immigration shopping:*** No country welcomes unreservedly the immigrants of all sorts. But, at the same time, there were always preferences for particular kinds of migrants and therefore some degree of immigration shopping. The 'welcome categories' of migrants include skilled workers, youth, good health, education and lack of dependents. Equally welcomed are the people who are business migrants, who bring wealth and jobs with them.

(c) ***Undocumented workers:*** The 'illegal' labour takes two predominant forms, overstaying and deliberate illegal entry. The first phenomenon reflects the increasingly practical difficulties of managing the turnstiles that turn increasingly fast as more and more people filethrough. There is good deal of leakage through the system as tourists, students and family visitors pass through the gates. Some violate in terms of their entry and work when they are not supposed to.

Second, there is increased evidence that there are organisations behind deliberate illegal entrants. Large sums of money change hands, entry certificates and visas are forged and border guards are bribed. Often, travel and shipping agents are involved.

(d) ***Skilled transients:*** Hidden from the history are the highly skilled international skilled migrants - professionals, construction engineers, consultants and otheRs Some of them are freelance, but most of them work for international companies.

(e) ***Unskilled contract workers:*** Unskilledd transients who are parallel to the skilled workers continue to arrive at foreign destinations. They are often exploited ruthlessly and are frequently used as a means to undercut the bargaining power of the better paid and organised workeRs The importing states intention is to avoid their permanent settlement.

(f) ***Women migrants:*** Sociologically, numerically and globally, the world has entered a new phase of female migration. This is characterised by independent movements in response to a demand for women to enter the global service economy. Some of this is in the sex industry, particularly in South-East Asia. Hostesses, sex workers and entertainers are required in significant numbers in countries such as Japan and are generally supplied from China and Thailand. Similarly, there is great demand for female domestic workers and maids in the Gulf countries and these women are supplied from Thailand, Philippines, Sri Lanka and India.

(vi) The major trends of global/international migration in modern times include the following:

- from all countries of the world to Israel,
- from all countries of the world to the United States of America and Western Europe,
- from the European countries to the U.S.,
- from colonised states to the colonial power states,
- from underdeloped to developed countries,
- from all countries of the world to Gulf states,
- from all countries of the world to Palestime by Jews,
- Mass migration from Pakistan to India and from India to Pakistan in 1947,
- KPs' migration from Kashmir to different parts of India and different countries of the world.

4. Regional Level Migration Trends

(i) These trends of migration occurred after the global level migration. So, following trends of migration can be associated with this particulat category:

- from one particular region to another particular region in the world,
- from various regions to other regions.

It also includes the following kinds of particular trends of migration:

- from Eastern Europe to Western Europe,
- from European countries to the United States,

- Tamil and Sri Lankan migrants to the Gulf states,
- South-East Asian Women migrants to Japan.

5. National-local Level Trends of Migration

This level of migration trends have been experienced within the national and sub-national territorial limits mostly in all developing and under-developed countries, especially in Asia and Africa. These kinds of migration in particular units occur in all classes, groups and communities in most of the countries. In quantitative terms, this type of migration trends attract the largest number of people within the national territories and qualitatively become a necessary pre-requsite for the broader and deeper process of overall change and development in the society. It also involves many general and particular socio-economic, cultural-political and other factors for its proper and solid initiation. In the pan-Indian society's background, this type of migration trends reflect in the following kinds of population movements:

- mass migration from rural areas to urban areas,
- from urban areas [cities and towns] to urban areas [cities and towns],
- from one state to other state/s in the country,
- from one particular region to other particular region,
- replacement migration in Kerala,
- mass labour migration to Panjab, J&K and Himachal Pradesh,
- socially stressful migration from Bihar and other states.

6. Patterns of Population Change

(i) The second prominent, dominant and most effective process of demographic transformation has been identified as different patterns of population change at the global level, i.e., in all countries of the world. This broader and deeper change has usually been recorded consistently and systematically in the census records in the recent past in all countries. It has been observed by the experts in the concerned field that this change was experienced at the global, regional and national levels.

(ii) Regarding population changes in the human society at the global level, David M. Heer, has observed that:

"Two separate frameworks of causal explanation are available for explaining world population growth. The first framework relates population to the means of subsistence. It is obvious the population of the world can be no greater than that number which can provide itself with a minimum subsistence from the world's resources. Since for most of the period in which human beings have inhabited this planet, the majority have lived very close to a minimum level of subsistence, major population increase has only been possible when the means of subsistence could be increased proportionately.

A second framework for examining the causes of world population increase is the examination of this increase in terms of its two components, the birth rate and death rate. On the worldwide basis, population can not increase unless the birth rate exceeds the death rate, and the greater the difference between the two rates [in favour of births, of course], the higher will be the rate of population growth. Analysis of world population growth from the standpoint of this framework focuses on factors leading to changes in birth and death rates.

In this thematic framework, various processes of demographic change can be explained and analysed. Heer explains this series of demographic changes in the following characteristics:

- changes in general distribution of world's population,
- changing process of mortality
- changing process of fertility
- changing pattern of migration
- population and social structure
- age-sex composition
- Population growth and economic development
- Population and political power
- Population legislation and policy

In the Indian context, the demographic transformation has been explained in terms of the changes in the following variables and factors:

- change in total population at-the national level
- the state level

- the regional level
- changes in distribution and density of population
- growth patterns in population
- migration patterns and trends
- changes in sex ratio
- changes in levels of literacy
- changes in the labour/work force

7. Trends of Migration and Pattern of Population Change

(i) The above explanation of different features of trends of migration and patterns of population change at the global, international, regional, national and local levels emerge as the dominant variables of demographic transformation. Both these demographic processes increase and intensify the other processes associated directly or indirectly with social transformation. Thus it can be argued that demographic transformation necessarily provided the basis for initiating the process of social transformation. In the following developments, this relationship leads to the reciprocal relationship between the processes of demographic and social transformations.

8. The Jammu and Kashmir Situation

(i) The above-mentioned theoretical-thematic background enables us to apply this framework in the case of demographic and social realities in the J&K state. In fact, in J&K after 1947, the following trends of migrtion were observed from time to time:

- Annual temporary Darbar-move migration from Jammu to Srinagar [In summer season] and

  From Srinagar to Jammu [in winter season] with official hierarchy, bureaucracy and government machinery for a period of six months;
- State to foreign countries like the U.S., Europe, Middle East, Gulf States and South East Asia by the local business fraternity for world famous Kashmiri handicraft business;
- State to state/s migration undertaken every year by small Kashmiri businessmen, traders, craftsmen, skilled labour for the sole economic purpose during the season;

- Significant degree of migration from the state to north Indian states of Panjab, Haryana, Himachal Pradesh, Chandigarh and Delhi by skilled, semi-skilled and unskilled labour during the winter season in Kashmir;
- In-migration of thousands of skilled, semiskilled and unskilled alien labour force to J&K throughout the year from the states of Bihar, Panjab, U.P., Rajasthan and Odisha. This unorganised labour migration has accumulated more than 3,00,000 outside labourers in the state in the last five decades and has developed potential political, economic, social and cultural implications;
- Seasonal migration of various kinds of skilled and semiskilled manpower during the turist season which starts from March and ends in October every year.
- Usual migration from 1947 onwards and mass migration in 1990-1991 of KPs from Kashmir to different cities and towns in the country and cities in foreign countries. This community of KPs made whole community-level migration in 1990 and have not returned so far despite various official and unofficial efforts and initiatives.

9. Different Patterns of Population Changes

(i) In this particular field also, the J&K state, after 1947, experienced various changes in the population. Most of these changes reveal in the following patterns:

- Changes in total population at the state level,
- Changes in the total population at the province level,
- Changes in the total population at the district level,
- Changes in the male-female and rural-urban composition of population in the state,
- Changes in the density and growth of total population in the state,
- Change in the birth and death rates in the state,
- Changes in age group composition in the state,
- Changes in the marital status of population in the state,
- Changes in the majority-minorities proportion in the population,

- Changes in the linguistic composition of population in the state, and
- Changes in the religious composition of population in the state.

10. Theme of this Book

(i) The scientific understanding and objective study of the demographic and social transformation in J&K after 1947 within the defined thematic and sociological framework stands the main objective of this book. Though this topic was of tremendous academic relevance and importance, not many studies were carried out inside as well as outside the state. The non-availability of demographic, especially of statistical nature, has created confusion and distortion regarding varios issues and problems involved. Dr Majid Hussain's edited book on social geography of J&K state (entitled) stood an exception in this regard. In fact, this book has provided the basic and necessary demographic information about J&K state.

(ii) This academic exercise has been carried out to provide the real, authentic, and relevant understanding of various issues and problems related directly or indirectly to this broader demographic theme. In reality, most of the papers included in this book were found highly relevant to the study of prevailing demographic situation in the J&K state, particularly in the Kashmir province. The special focus on the Kashmir situation stands predetermined as it fulfills the primary objective of the book. However, at every stage of explanation, the wholistic picture of the entire state has not been lost.

11. Specific Context of Methodology

(i) This book consists four empirical studies and 12 research papers based on primary and secondary sources. These studies were carried out and research papers were written at different times, with different objectives and with different perspectives. So, different methodologies were applied in different academic writings. It follows that distinct methods and techniques were used in different studies and papers in order to understand, explain and interpret various facets of demographic and social transformation in J&K.

(ii) The methodology of four empirical studies have been fully explained in their respective chapters, as mentioned below:

- KP migration (chapter 5),
- Labour migration (chapter 6),
- Increasing suicides (chapter 12), and
- Late marriages (chapter 13).

(iii) On the other hand, the rest of the research papers are based on the primary and secondary source official-non-official documents, census records, books, journals and newspapeRs These sources were used rationally and objectively and according to the academic needs of these research papeRs Further details below clarify these points.

(iv) While the universe of study of four particular case studies was the Kashmir province in the J&K state, which composed of formerly six and now ten districts. In all other research papers, the universe of study was the entire state, which composed of formerly 14 and now 22 districts. The data about these districts have been taken mainly from census records of all decades (except in 1951 and 1991) at the district and sub-district levels.

(v) While in the case empirical case studies, the methods/techniques of questionnaire and interview were used to gather the required information by the trained research investigatoRs In addition, the observation method also helped in collecting authentic data-information from the field. These and other related details of methodology can be studied in their respective chapteRs

(vi) In the cases of research papers, primary sources such as official documents, particularly census records of 1941-2011, unofficial documents and other related sources were used first. Subsequently, secondary sources such as books, papers from journals, and articles from newspapers were also used.

(vii) After collecting data and information from primary and secondary sources in both kinds of research, these were aggregated, tabulated and analysed according to the themes and objectives of various studies. Thus in all cases, the main propositions were developed and conclusions arrived at through the above-mentioned methodologies.

SECTION A : GLOBAL, NATIONAL AND REGIONAL TRENDS OF MIGRATION

2

Global Migration and Globalisation: The Kashmir Case

1. Global Migration

(i) Migration generally refers to the movement of human beings from one place to another. It occurs at regional as well as universal levels and in all societies irrespective of differences in their regions, cultures, religions, languages, social structures as well as economic and political systems. Sociologically, it reflects three primary and crucial features. First, it refers to the movement of human beings from one particular place of residence to another place of residence over a period of time and having certain definite reasons to do so. Second, it includes debasement of unit of residence at one place and subsequent establishment of another unit of residence at other place. Third, it represents the phenomenon which engulfs entire life of people concerned as they change their life-pattern wholly.

The initiation of the process of migration on this globe may be traced to the earliest human beings. The earliest human society may be the society of 'Adam' and 'Eve' and their offspring who had to move from place to place. As has been studied by sociologists, demographers and other concerned experts, human migration had certain causes which can be explained in terms of 'push and pull' factoRs While the 'push' factors refer to numerous reasons of migration (which are involuntary in nature), such as search for food, security, favourable climate and safety from various epidemic diseases and calamities, the 'pull' factors point to several reasons (which are voluntary in nature) that include desire for change and improvement in the quality of life.

(ii) Patterns and Factors of International Migration:

In the background of human migration from antiquity from one place to another place, certain specific patterns of migration have emerged in human history. Equally important is the fact that these patterns of migration can be related to specific causes. Thus, sociologists and demographers have developed a co-relation between patterns and factors of migration which may be explained as follows:

(i) Climatic - from cold to hot places, hot to temperate places; and from hills to plains.

(ii) Political-from one to another country, near or far away.

(iii) Economic-from developing to developed world; and from rest of the world to the Gulf.

(iv) Religious-from rest of the world to Israel; and from India to Pakistan and vice versa.

(v) Cultural-from rest of the world to U.S. and Europe.

(vi) Educational-from Asia and Africa to the U. S. and Western Europe.

It has also been observed that migration had set implications on the migrant as well as host societies. Most important consequences are as follows : First, migration creates a significant demographic change in host societies which reflects in their changing composition and fertility-mortality rates. In Kuwait and Malaysia, migrants have changed the population composition radically. While in the former case, the migrants compose 55 per cent of the total population, the latter's proportion of migrant Chinese population has gone up to near 50 per cent of the total population. Second, migration gives rise to plurality of cultures, religions, languages, social structures and, more importantly, ethnicity. The case of ethnic communities in most of the countries in the world reveals this phenomenon. Third, with the growth of plurality, there emerges problems of competition, conflict, control and so on. Fourth, mass migration gives rise to new societies and new civilisations. The case of America is a distinctive example in this regard. The famous sociologist of Iran, Dr. Ali Shariati, concluded on the basis of his study of human societies that all 27 civilisations which are known ot the human society today were preceded by the processes of mass migraton in this connection. he cites the examples of Christian, Jewish and Islamic civilisations.

(iii) Three major Streams of Global Migration:

Experts have identified three distinctive streams of migration. First, in the context of change and development at the global level, significant number of people from the developing world migrated to the developed countries in the world, particularly to the United States and Western Europe for economic, educational, social and other material reasons. Majority of such migrations comprised people of higher education, professionals, technicians and experts in different fields as well as skilled and semi-skilled personnel. Though the migration initiated in the medieval times, it experienced a sharp increase in modern times.

Second, people from whole of world, developed as well as developing, moved to the tiny states in the Gulf primarily for economic reasons. After oil was discovered in the Gulf in the sixties, the region witnessed large-scale migration from Asia, particularly the Indo-Pak sub-continent. The migrants included professionals, technicians, skilled labour and experts in different fields from developed countries and semi-skilled and unskilled labour from developing countries. While in the former case, the majority of migrants settled in developed countries and adopted their culture partly or wholly, migrants in the latter case stayed there for as short period as possible to adopt the host's culture.

Third, another stream of migration in the contemporary times took place in most of the states in Asia, Africa and Latin America at the time when their colonisation ended or was nearing its end. In this type of migration, people migrated within their nation states from rural to urban areas for economic and other reasons. The most important reason for this migration was the colonial-type of development which focused on urban areas at the cost of rural areas to benefit the colonial ruleRs This type of migration took place in majority of developing— third world—countries and could not be avoided in the environment created by the type of economy pursued by governments in these states. While this type of migration led to rural dependence, continuity of rural under-development and exploitation of rural resources, it also contributed to demographic change, economic inequality and multi-dimensional problems of migrants in urban areas. While majority of migrants in this process settled in urban areas, minority of them either shifted to rural areas or moved from rural to urban areas and *vice versa.*

2. Globalisation

The concept of 'globalisation' specifically refers to "all those processes by which the peoples of the world are incorporated into a single society, global society."[1] These processes are long in making an impact on different locations, countries, groups and individuals in a highly uneven manner. They have increased in scope and intensity, and in the recent past, this has happened at an accelerating rate. Thus, it can be seen as a "set of mutually reinforcing transformations that are occurring more or less simultaneously."[2] No single one of these is necessarily more important than the otheRs In this context, we are in a position to identify six main features of 'Globalisation' which follows hereunder:

- Changing concepts of space and time;
- An increasing volume of cultural interactions;
- The commonality of problems facing all the world's inhabitants;
- Growing interconnections and interdependencies;
- A network of increasingly powerful transnational actors and organisations; and
- The synchronisation of all the dimensions involved in globalisation.[3]

3. The International Migrants

(i) The international migrants constitute an important part in the phenomenon of globalisation. Robin Cohen presents the argument that they "take advantage of the interdependence of the world's economies and find themselves a place, sometimes a very modest place, in the global labour market."[4]

In actuality, they were active agents of globalisation, establishing a dense network of connections between their places of origin and places of settlement. Although there are relatively few international migrants compared with internal or national migrants, their movements stood highly sensitive and crucial in importance.[5] It seems that through inertia, social involvement with a natal community, lack of opportunity, immigration restrictions and xenophobia, the numbers actually crossing international borders for the purpose of settlement are restrained. For example, in Western Europe, the percentage of foreigners to locals was 1.3 per cent in 1950. This had more than trebled by 1990, but the last number still represents a very small diminution of homogeneity of

European states compared with the massive inroads of globalisation in other states. [6]

4. Post-war Global Trends of Migration

(i) After the Second World War, labour migration was observed mainly from South to North, i.e., from former colonial territories to their old metropolis, or from adjacent poor countries to their richer neighbouRs Turks and Yuguslavs went to Germany, while Maxicans came to the USA in greater numbeRs In the 1970s, industrialised countries of Europe and North America attracted the labour migrants for permanent settlement. Following that trend, several new forms of international migration became evident during last few decades such as the mass migration to the Gulf states from industrialised as well as from under-developed Asian and African countries. The following six major trends/streams of labour migration at the global level were observed[7]:

(a) ***Growth of Refugee Migration:*** The general estimates reveal that the current number of refugees at the global level is 18-20 million people. The Genneva Convention in 1951 has given a legal definition according to which he/she stands as someone who is fleeing from a real threat of persecution in their country of their origin on the grounds of their background or political opinion. A 'refugee' can be differentiated from an 'asylum-seeeker' who claims for refugee status but have not been recognised and from 'internally displaced person' who has been pushed from his/her normal place of residence by War, civil conflict or an ecological disaster. With the end of war in Kosovo, the U.N. High Commission has been charged with the responsibility of resettling about half a million Kosovos. Based on previous experience of the 1980s, if refugees are dispersed far from their homelands only about 25 per cent return later on. However, given that most of the Kosovos are in camps just across the border, the majority is expected to resettle in their native province. At the same time, the bulk of the Serb minority in Kosovo was expected to flee to Serbia proper.[8]

(b) ***Immigration Shopping:*** The fact stands that no country in the world unreservedly welcomes immigrants of all sorts. There have been formal and informal instructions on immigration for over a century, often on racial grounds. But, at the same time, there were always preferences for particular kinds of migrants and therefore

some degree of immigration shopping was preferred. At present, no country wants any and all immigrants, but many want small numbers of particular ones. They have linked their economic, manpower and immigration departments structurally and are intent of finding special kinds of migrants to fill slots. In reality, what these countries want are skills, youth, good health, education, lack of dependence and specialisation. Equally welcomed are so-called 'business migrants' who bring wealth and possibly jobs to host countries.[9]

(c) ***Undocumented Workers:*** The illegal labour has taken two predominant forms, overstaying and illegal entry. First, this phenomenon reflects the increasingly practical difficulties of managing the turnstiles than turn increasingly fast as more and more people file through. There is a good deal of leakage through the system as tourists, students and family visitors pass through the gates. Some violate the terms of their entry and work when they were not supposed to. Others stay on after their entry visas were expired. Second, there was increased evidence of organisation behind deliberate illegal entrants. Large sums of money change hands, entry certificates and visas are forged and border guards are bribed. Often travel and shipping agents are involved. There was also some degree of frequent complicity of employers who wanted cheap labour with particular skills and qualities.[10]

(d) ***Women Migrants:*** It is argued that sociologically the world has entered a new phase of female migration. This was characterised by independent movements in response to a demand for women to enter the global service economy. Some of this was in sex industry, particularly in South-East Asia. Hostesses, sex workers and entertainers are requireds in significant numbers in countries such as Japan and are generally supplied from China and Thailand. Similarly, there was great demand for female domestic servants and maids in the Gulf countries and these women were supplied fromThailand, Philippines, Sri Lanka and India. In addition to brides, maids and domestic workers, there were waitresses, casual staff at fast food outlets, nurses, secretaries, hotel receptionist, worker of hospitality industry, stewardesses, cleaners and others were required in these neo-rich countries. According to an estimate, women now compose majority of international migrants. These markets are driven from both sides. On the supply side, the governments regard labour exports much like any other export

which is a foreign currency earner. On the demand side, changes in gender power and status in Western and other countries had a significant impact.[11]

(e) ***Skilled Transients:*** Hidden from history were the highly skilled international migrants, i.e., professionals, technocrats, computer experts, doctors, business managers, construction engineers, consultants and othet specialists. But, majority among them worked for international companies for limited periods of the contract and returned to their countries of origin. This type of international migrants were called 'skilled transients', 'sojournes' and 'denizens' in the sense of priviledged ones and preferred ones.

(f) ***Unskilled Contract Workers:*** Unskilled migrants too arrived in huge numbers at foreign destinations. They were often manipulated and exploited and were frequently used as a means to undercut the bargaining power of the better paid, highly qualified-trained and properly skill-based. The importing states' intension was to avoid their permanent settlement in their countries and so were comparatively harsh and strict with them and their documents. The situation like this emerged in the Gulf states after 1990s when they developed their own expertise and experienced manpower partly and unskilled workers were treated harshly and sent back to their homes.[12]

5. Relationship between Global Migration and Global Society

(i) The above grand-level theoretical formulations reveal a close relationship between globalisation and international migration which is characterised by one-sided and both-sided impacts. While international migration necessarily results in many aspects of globalisation, it too effects various trends/pattern of global movement. In this situational background, certain international and national factors equally played a decisive role in the initiation and intensification of the processes of globalisation and international migration. This emerges as the sociological reality in many societies.

6. The Indian Situation of Migration

(i) A similar situation prevailed in the case of migration in India after independence. Several types of migration-patterns emerged in post-colonial India. First, linear migration which involved people who moved from rural to urban areas and settled there. Second, cyclical migration which involved people who moved from rural to urban areas and back. This process took place repeatedly. Third, migration from rural-urban areas of one place to urban areas of other place. This involved people who felt compelled to migrate due to political, religious, ethnic and other such factoRs The migration of people from India to Pakistan and vice versa in 1947-48 and Kashmiri Pandits from Kashmir to different parts of J&K state and India in 1990-91 fit in this type of migration.

(ii) The causation of these and other types of migration in post-colonial India can be explained in the rural and urban context. In the rural context, modernisation of agriculture led to unprecedented increase in production benefitting significant number of rural people. But, at the same time, this process created the problem of unemployment in rural areas. These rural unemployed people had no alternative except to move to the cities in search of livelihood. In the urban context, various processes of modernisation, especially educational and job opportunities compelled the people to migrate. Moreover, the processes of urbanisation, industrialisation, development of secular, materialistic and individualistic outlook attracted, on the one hand, people from rural to urban areas and, on the other, made preferable for some people to migrate from one to other urban areas.

7. The Migration Patterns in Kashmir

(i) As has happened in all societies of the world, the Kashmiri society too has undergone this process with far reaching implications. In the ancient times, people of different races came to Kashmir and some of them settled here. In the medieval times, Kashmir experienced the processes of in-migration and out-migration. In the former case, many aliens, especially Mughals, Afghans, Sikhs and Dogras, came here as rulers and many of them settled here. Again, thousands of missionaries came from several parts of Central Asia, converted the locals to Islam peacefully and majority of them settled here. In the case of out-migration, thousands of locals had to move outside Kashmir primarily for political reasons. During that period, the locals, both Muslims and Hindus, were compelled to migrate to different parts of India, especially to northern and central India. Pandit Jawaharlal Nehru and Sir Mohammad Iqbal represented such migrant communities.

(ii) In the modern times, the Kashmiri society underwent the processes of in-migration and out-migration. While the former was less significant, the latter was more significant. In the first case, some tiny groups such as several professional-occupational groups, bureaucrats and so on came here and settled here. On the other hand, out-migration started from early decades of the 20th century and that was intensified after 1947. This may explain the out-migration of KPs from Kashmir to different parts of India from early decades of the last century for educational and employment purposes.[13]

(iii) The KP community was a near-total literate community and individual of this community was after government job which was not possible in the changed situation at that time. The KPs with their higher technical and professional qualifications, could not be accommodated in the state as it was under-developed at that time. The Kashmiri Muslims [KM] got education from early decades of this century, especially after 1947, and subsequently shared the government jobs with the KPs. In this situation, the process of migration among the KPs intensified from 1947 who settled in different urban areas in India. This explains the phenomenon of the presence of KPs in most of the cities of India on top positions in all fields, especially bureaucracy, education, business and industry.[14]

(iv) The phenomenon of KP migration from Kashmir has parallel examples in the Indian society. In Tamil Nadu, the Tamil Brahmins occupied higher status and top positions in the bureaucracy in pre-independent days. As a result of the exploitative role of Brahmin caste traditionally, the Dravida Kazagam [DK] movement started in the 1930s under the leadership of Periyar to destroy the Brahmanic hegemony. Thus, after 1947, all DK parties in Tamil Nadu which came to power there, made efforts to debase the traditional Brahmanic hegemony in the administration. Consequently, most of the Brahmins had to leave the state and settle in different parts of India, especially Delhi.[15]

(v) Kashmir experienced a radical type of migration in 1989-90 when the KPs made a near-total movement to different cities of India, especially in the north. Subsequently, the KMs too migrated, but in lesser numbeRs Despite the fact that 90-95 per cent of KPs migrated from Kashmir, this was caused mainly by political factoRs The religious factor is not primary but co-incidental. The impact of this migration has been negative and disintegrative, though the community opted for this type of migration.[16]

7. International Migration and Kashmir

(i) In the context of Kashmir, the phenomena of globalisation in kashmir and international migration were experienced simultaneously and because of local factors such as alien rule in Kashmir before 1947 and to achieve educational mobility by locals after 1947.[17] Subsequently, the involvement of global factors such as emergence of oil economy in the Gulf states in the 1970s and the highest salaries for skilled and semi-skilled personnel there, was experienced. After some time, both processes of globalisation and international migration entered in to a reciprocal relationship due to global, regional and local factoRs This relatioinship was highly intensified in the following period.

(ii) In the sociological framework suggested by Robin Cohen,[18] the relevant situation in Kashmir revealed three particular aspects, which may be characterised as:

(a) growth of refugee population,

(b) migration of skilled transients, and

(c) migration of unskilled contract workeRs

Other three aspects of immigration shopping, migration of undocumented workers and migration of women workers were not experienced in the Kashmir case. So, we may explain the former set of three factors only.

(iii) First, international migration was experienced in the contemporary history of Kashmir because more powerful outside forces invaded, captured and ruled the territory and most often vocal locals were compelled to migrate outside. In the mediaval and modern times, the Mughal, Afghan, Sikh and Dogra rulers, who captured and ruled Kashmir forcefully, created conditions in which vocal sections of society were compelled to leave Kashmir and settle outside their country. Thus we observe many such migrant communities living in different areas of the Indian sub-continent. Even in the post-partition period, Kashmir experienced out-migration of the Kashmiri Pandits to national and international destinations for educational, employment and other economic opportunities. In the recent past, a mass out-migration of the KPs was experienced in 1990-1991 due to political factor. As a result, lakhs of KPs were forced to leave their place of residence and live the refugee life in Jammu and other cities of the country.

(iv) The author's study of this migration[19] revealed that due to 100 per cent literacy and higher standards of technical and professional education, the migration had helped them in their shift to foreign countries. On the other hand, the Kashmiri Maslims, after migrating from Kashmir, too had migrated to foreign countries for business, higher education and other purposes, especially to Western Europe, the U.S., Middle East and Gulf states, and South-East Asian countries. Many Kashmiri skilled and semi-skilled personnel such as doctors, engineers, computer experts, accountants, managers and unskilled workers too migrated to the Gulf states and stayed there for different periods of time. Many of them still stay there and work despite hard conditions and uncertainty of their future. Added to these types of migration from Kashmir, there has been largescale international migration from Pak-administered-Kashmir to different areas in Britain, especially to Birmingham, Luton and Manchester. They compose mainly of skilled, semi-skilled and unskilled labour force and have established huge ethnic community in that country.

(v) The nature and enormity of international migration in itself reflects significant degree of globalisation related to the Kashmiri society. The local international migrants became active and indigeneous agents of globalisation, establishing network of community connections between their places of origin and places of settlement. At the same time, the situation arising out of short-term and long-term implications of modern science, technology and development certainly led to initiation, intensification enlargement of several processes of globalisation, particularly the universal impact of information technology. Subsequently, the media revolution created the functional component parts of the 'global village' which reflected in social, cultural, economic, educational, religious, political and other fields. Finally, the political developments in Indian-administered Kashmir could also be related directly or indirectly to the global impact in this concerned field.

(vi) The cumulative effect of most of the processes of globalisation and international migration has also led to the emergence of "Kashmiri Diaspora" which maintains consciously and strengthens deliberately the contact and impact between their place of origin and place/s of settlement. It has also given birth to strong functional social entities in the U.S. [especially in New York, Pheldelphia and Chicago], Western Europe, particularly Britain [especially London, Luton, Birmingham and Manchester], Middle Eastern countries (especially Gulf states of Saudi Arabia, Kuwait, and U. A.E.), and South East Asian countries (especially Malaysia, Hong Kong and Singapore). A significant number of these Kashmiri migrants composed of doctors, engineers, managers, accountants, secretaries, while others were semi-skilled and non-skilled workeRs The dominant majority of these transient migrants were composed of males and singles [unmarried or families left at home]. Very less number of Kashmiri migrants were females as they generally don't prefer regular and remunerative jobs in foreign countries. Nearly all these migrants have legal documents like visas and contract papers and have entered those countries with legal and valid documents. The sole motive of this out and international migration at its initial stage was economic and still remains so. Though they follow all global trends of culture, they maintain their original identity at the social, cultural and political level. In actuality, the have proved as 'radiators' of some prominent features of global social life. While majority of Kashmiri migrants from Indian-administrated-Kashmir were professionals, technocrats, and skilled workers and had higher educational qualifications, most of the Kashmiri migrants from Pak-administered-Kashmir were semi-skilled or non-skilled workers and with lower educational qualifications.

References

1. Manfred B. Stager, Globalisation : A Very Short Introduction (New York, 2003, Oxford), p. 8.
2. *Ibid.*
3. Robin Cohen and Paul Kennedy, Global Sociology (New York, 2000, Macmillan), p. 26.
4. *Ibid.*
5. *Ibid.*
6. See Anand Kumar, Understanding Globalisation and Indian Society (New Delhi, 2011, Palm Leaf Publications).
7. See Cohen and Kennedy, op. cit., No. 3.
8. See Cohen and Kennedy, op. cit., No. 3.
9. *Ibid.*
10. *Ibid.*
11. *Ibid.*
12. *Ibid.*
13. See B.A. Dabla, Sociological Implications of Pandit Migration in J & K (Srinagar, 2008, JK Books).
14. *Ibid.*

15. See B.A. Dabla, "Globalisation and its Impact on Kashmir" (paper presented in a national seminar on Challenges of Globalisation: Sociology organised by Department of Sociology, University of Kashmir, Srinagar in October 2008).
16. B.A. Dabla, op. cit., No. 13.
17. *Ibid.*
18. See Robin Cohin, op. cit., No. 3.
19. *Ibid.*

3

Some National and Regional Trends of Migration in India and Their Social Context

1. Introduction

1.1. The process of migration essentially represents the pan-Indian phenomenon and reflected in different trends/patterns in different regions, states and areas. Equally important stands the fact that all these micro and macro-level processes occurred in and effected the concerned social context. It follows that migration was triggered in all states of India by various social, economic, political, educational and cultural factors and, subsequently, effected the migrants' life conditions [in their places of work and places of residence] as well as the lives of hosts/employeRs Thus the crucial social developments determined the nature and migration pattern of throughout the country, though different in intensity and degree, in the last decades. For example, poor people from rural areas in the state of Bihar usually migrated to other regions and states in the country mainly due to poverty conditions and social oppression of upper castes. This particularly effected the migrant's economic life at their places of work and residence. Moreover, as a result of constant interaction between migrants and local-employers were effected mostly adversely and it generally gave rise to hostilities and antagonism between these two involved communities. Thus the presence and work of migrants gave rise to certain serious problems and issues, which they had to think about seriously and put before their resolution. In this background, it may be argued that the state to state or region to region migration patterns in India in recent decades were determined by the immediate social context [in terms of push and pull factors] and also effected the life conditions of migrants and locals-employers and their relationship in its social context again. This theme will be further elucidated in the following sections.

2. **Pan-Indian Migration Trends**

2.1. The phenomenon of inter-state and inter-region migration of labour force came to the fore in the wake of incidents of violence against migrants in southern states of India recently. In the broader and deeper context, neoliberal policy and low investment in agriculture and rural infrastructure in the globalisation framework led to mass migration from rural to urban areas in all states in search of employment and livelihood. An expert explains this impact in the following words:

"Migration is known to have diverse impacts on growth and development, on migrants and their households, and on the social and political life prevalent in the source and destination areas. These impacts are complex and run in different directions.[1]

2.2 According to a National Sample Survey [NSS], the trend of migration stands relatively 'little'. In the year 2007-2008, there were less than 30.00 per cent of the people in India were considered as migrants.[2] The proportion of migrants was higher in urban areas [i.e., 35.00 per cent] than in rural areas [i.e., 26.00 per cent].[3] The male migration rate was far lower than the female one, in both rural and urban areas. In rural areas, nearly 48.00 per cent of the females were migrants as against 5.00 per cent of the males. In urban areas, the male migration rate was about 26.00 per cent as compared with 46.00 per cent of the females.[4]

2.3. Dominated as Marriage the cause of migration for women with 91.00 per cent of rural women and 61.00 per cent urban women participating in this process. This was also reflected in the geographical nature of the movement, about 90.00 per cent of rural and 80.00 per cent of the urban women moved within the state of origin.[5] For men, the most important factor for migration was 'employment', with 29.00 per cent of rural male migrants and 56.00 per cent of urban male migrants.[6]

2.4. The survey also found that migration in India was associated positively with income and social status. Overall, migration was found to be the lowest for the bottom 10.00 per cent of the population in terms of expenditure class in both rural and urban areas. All over the country, the migration rate was lowest among non-literates and highest for those with the educational qualifications of graduation and above.[7]

2.5. Village studies conducted recently in different parts of the country clearly suggest that some of the recent migration has been because of pull factors, particularly the increase in construction sector activities. A substantial part of internal migration, both long-term and short-term, is also distress-led movement. It has been driven by lack of rural employment generation, economic difficulties of cultivation and inadequate employment opportunities in towns.[8]

2.6. The migration these types of implication of on migrants and their families has been explained as mentioned below:

"Not only do migrant children have to experience continuing flux and insecurity, but they also typically deal with very harsh material conditions - lack of adequate nutrition and sanitation and little access to public health and education facilities. They are often drawn into the workforce at very early age and in very unsavoury conditions.[9]

2.7. In another relevant observation, it was revealed that:

"Any objective assessment would show that contemporary migration is linked to increasing urbanisation triggered by the pursuit of neoliberal economic policies and globalisation. Consequently, it has linkages to the stagnation of agriculture and the agrarian economy... Even the 2011 Census data underscore this, recording a higher growth in urban population as compared to the rural population. This displacement from homestead and the social, cultural and economic alienation amidst new urban surroundings along with the stress, creates in the receiving urban centres, add up to the creation and explosion of social tensions. Factors ranging from racial discrimination to social ostracisation to sexual discrimination and harassment spurt in these situations.[10]

3. The Causation of this Situation

3.1. This pan-Indian demographic situation, mentioned above, can be related to seven sets of broader reasons, which were identified by the Census of India [2011] and National Sample Survey [NSS], which include the following:

[i] work and employment related,

[ii] business,

[iii] education,

[iv] marriage,

[v] moved at birth,

[vi] moved with family, and

[vii] other reasons.[11]

3.2. Both the assessments revealed that only about 3.00 per cent of the Indian people have changed their "usual place of residence" for employment-related reasons. But, the comparative analysis of two enumerations also shows that "32.00 per cent of all inter-State migrants during 1991 - 2001 migrated for the reason of work or employment. Other relevant studies of this migration have noticed the movement of household accounts for about 0.00 per cent of the inter-State migrants.[12]

3.3. Another assessment in 2007-2008 estimated that 141 million [minus seasonal migrant] workers or 30.90 per cent of the Indian workforce could be classified as total number of migrants. This proves clearly that employment-related migration is growing, particularly in urban areas. However, other groups such as poorer migrants in the informal sector, short-duration seasonal and circular migrants deserve special focus because they belong to the vulnerable sections of the working poor.[12A]

3.4. These demographic developments have taken place in many states especially Uttar Pradesh [U.P.], Bihar, Chhattisgarh and Uttarakhand, which have recorded relatively higher rates of labour migration over past several decades. In the last decade, there has been a significant increase in labour migration from the north-eastern States. According to a study in 2011, higher rates of migration were noticed from this region to different regions in the country. The number of migrants had increased 12 times in the last five years While in 2005, there was the movement of estimated 34,000 migrants, it had reached to the level of 4,14,850 in 2010 from this region. If the current rates/trends of migration continued unabated, it will lead to the number of 50,00,000 in the next five years from this particular region.[13]

3.5. U.P. Migrants from who form about 35.00 per cent of labour migrants in the country in the past 18 months have also faced discrimination and encountered hostility and antagonism like in Maharastra, the most preferred destination of the migrants in the state.[14] Bihar Labour migrants from flocked to Panjab, J&K, Delhi and other north Indian states as a response to the labour scarcity and the competition among farmers there. However, this Bihari labour force in these alien states was treated undesirably and was targeted for racial discrimination and social differentiation. Even they became the targets of minor and major attacks and violence. In other studies, it was revealed that there was massive influx of migrant labour from Orrisa, U.P., and Bihar in to booming construction industry in the whole country.

3.6. A unique case of migration and its reverse trend was observed in the case of Assam. One can imagine about the degree of out-migration from Assam from the fact that estimated 20 lakh job-seekers were registered with employment exchanges, who can migrate any time in future.[14A] It was further observed that "these young people, particularly the security guards and others whose stakes are not very high in the cities where they work, might want to return when they are ready to marry and settle down. The money they earn may not be enough to marry on in those cities, and they might think of their hometowns as a better option where they may be able to use the experience they have acquired.... If such a reverse migration is sought to be prevented, then governments in the region must get in to touch with the employers of these young people and negotiate on their behalf for better wages and ensure that they can avail themselves of security schemes such as pension and insurance."[15]

4. Migration from Bihar

4.1. In the case of Bihar, which stands backward in many fields, social security systems such as government educational institutions, public health care facilities and public distribution system have failed to benefit the larger people, migration has become a powerful mechanism for social mobility and progress. The absence of land reforms has led to a deeply unequal society in the agrarian society in the state. Whereas upper-castes own most of the agricultural lands, other backward castes/classes [OBC] and Dalits have hardly any land of their own. As such, majority of temporary migrants from Bihar are landless labourers and work for meager wages for their work at landlords' farms. Thus economic distress and caste exploitation are two factors that drove the poor villagers to migrate to other states. That is why the backward class population in Bihar stood as the largest group of migrant workforce in India.

4.2. According to the 2001 census reports, around 1.7 million people from Bihar had migrated in the decade 1991-2001.[16] Another related survey revealed that the Bihari labour force migrated to the following states and in the proportion mentioned below:

- Punjab 26.36 per cent of the total
- Delhi 21.34 per cent of the total
- Maharashtra 15.06 per cent of the total
- West Bengal 05.86 per cent of the total[17]

4.3. It has been observed that every type of migration in the national context has emerged as a strong social leveller in Bihar. So, while it has created chances for overall mobility and enabled the migrants to come out against the traditional pattern of exploitation in the villages. An observer has made the following statement in this regard:

"The added income through temporary migration has given Dalits and OBCs a collective voice to speak up against the landlords, who have historically exploited them economically and socially. The decreased dependence on landlords and exposure to big cities, where caste based exploitation is not overt, have enabled the migrants to develop different vocational skills.[18]

Moreover, in the traditional Bihari society, the women were never allowed to work on the agricultural fields. But, after the migrants' adopted new attitudes, this traditional pattern of behaviour has experienced a significant change. As a result, the women now either work on the lands in the absence of their men or accompany their men to the places of work. Thus women's mobility has changed her status and role to a maximum degree, if not in totality.[19]

4.4. It has also been experienced that the Muslim minority community, which form 18.00 per cent of the total population in Bihar in 2011, has improved significantly its economic conditions due to migration and working in all sorts of jobs, considered menial, lower status or otherwise. While a significant number of the Bihari unskilled labour force migrated to the Gulf states, rest of them migrated to other state in India, especially J&K, Panjab, Maharashtra and Delhi. It was specifically observed that:

"Services such as vehicle repairing, whitewashing, wall plastering, tailoring and plumbing came to be identified as occupations of Muslims. In metropolitan cities, these are relatively well paid jobs. Taking advantage of this, lower Middle class Muslims have started to migrate in large numbers from Katihar, Kishengunj and Araria districts, where they form more than half the population. Migration has significantly improved the position of Muslims in north Bihar, so much so that the BJP is adopting a hard Hinduvta position whenever it finds a chance."[20]

4.5. It is the same social and economic background in which the Bihari Muslim labourers migrated in large numbers to the state of J&K, especially to the Kashmir province, which stands the only Muslim-majority state in the country. In this case also, the overall conditions of the migrant labour force improved significantly after working several years or decades in Kashmir. It has revealed clearly in a study that the migrants from Bihar, whose number was estimated unofficially at about 3,00,000 in the entire Kashmir valley and some other districts in the Jammu region,[21] improved their life conditions tremendously at their places of work and in their households back home.[22] The new style and standard among the Bihari Muslims reflected in their consumption pattern, education, dress patterns, food habits, bank deposits, expenditure on health care, construction of residential houses in rural and urban areas and other such developments, which was completely unprecedented and unconventional.[23]

5. Hostilities between Migrants and Hosts

5.1. As has happened in the past, and repeated in Banglore on a day when 30,000 migrants from the north-eastern states had to leave the city,[24] the migrants were not appreciated at all places and by all occupational groups, religious communities, castes and classes. As a result of this antagonistic relationship for relatively a longer time, there develop a kind of hostilities between the two and prolong for some time. This situation ideally exists in the metropolitan city of Mumbai which is characterised as the "migrant city" and is the home of 124 lakh people in which there is a tiny section of 'locals' as per census records.[25] The arrival and accumulation of lakhs of migrants in the city has led to the negative reaction by the locals and infuriated the political parties and organisations. The political role of the Shiv Sena can be analysed in this context. This has culminated in political hostilities and political problems and sometimes it resulted in violent incidents.[26]

6. Plurality and Diversity of Migrants

6.1. The migrant population stands diverse in terms of class, region and ethnicity, with people coming from different states such as Bihar, Orissa, West Bengal and north-eastern region. A large section of migrant labourers especially employed in unorganised sector live in one-room accommodations in dingy, unhygienic localities while its cheap labour keeps the wheels of the economy running. Indeed, migration is sometimes experienced as liberation from old prejudices and cultural complexities. Thus migration comes with its own set of insecurities.[27] Thus diversity and plurality creates dissension and downward trends in material life. But, in the larger context, it has proved beneficial and emancipator.

7. **Replacement Migration in Kerala**

7.1. The number of Kerala migrants living abroad at present is about 2.28 million. Another 1.15 million migrants have returned after working abroad. There are other 3.43 million non-resident Keralites and another 9.31 lakh Kerala migrants living in other states of India.[28] At the earlier stage, the majority of emigrants were mostly skilled or semi-skilled workers and other non-agricultural labourers with low educational attainments, and their exit helped to ease the unemployment problem partly. However, their remittances were used mostly to spur the construction boom and not productive ventures. Consequently, there was decline in area under agriculture and in farm production and loss of jobs in agriculture.[29]

7.2. Meanwhile, due to scarcity of labour, the wage rates in construction and other manual jobs remained comparatively high in Kerala. A lot of these migrants came from the neighbouring states in the 1970s onwards. The profile of these migrants has changed considerably in the last decade. In fact, the early migrants in the state of Kerala were mainly from Tamil Nadu, Karnataka, West Bengal, Orissa, Bihar, Assam, U.P., Chhattisgarh and Uttrakhand. This migrant labour included the following categories:

- Construction workers,
- Casual labourers,
- Road workers
- Semi-skilled carpenters,
- Semi-skilled masons,
- Plumbers,
- Electricians,
- Farm workers,
- Domestic helpers, and
- Hotel employees,
- Jewellery workers,
- Cashew processing workers,
- Plywood unit workers;
- Workers at quarries, petrol stations, slaughter houses and brick kilns.[30]

7.3. Unlike their counterparts in Kerala, these workers were willing to do any work, their labour was cheaper, they worked for long hours, and they were considered a 'decent lot'. This represented the general refrain favouring the increasing and silent inflow of migrants into the states from near-by as well as from far-off states. This trend of migrant labourers has been characterised as the "replacement migration".[31]

7.4. A recent study of the Centre for Development studies [CDS], Thiruvananthapuram concluded as follows:

"Emigration of workers from Kerala, demographic contraction of the supply of young workers brought about by the rapid demographic transition in the State, the higher wages charged by Kerala's workers, the ability of Kerala workers to sustain themselves with remittances from relatives even without work for long periods, the reluntance on the part of Kerala workers to do hard physical work - all these have endangered the era of replacement migration in Kerala."[32]

Other studies by the CDS indicate that the disparity between the wage rates in Kerala and in the Gulf states is narrowing. It was because of that reason that there was a discernible decline in the number of emigrants from Kerala.

"One study conducted in the United Arab Emirates [UAE] among 1,000 unskilled workers, found the average monthly wage among them to be Rs 11,869, whereas the daily wage for a Keralite worker within the State is already as high as Rs 450. Migrant labourers are willing to work for lower wages, Rs 320 to Rs 350 a day, which are substantially higher than the wages in their own states."[33]

7.5. In the recent years, wherever migrants bring their families too along with them, Kerala is witnessing the reintroduction of child labour. Though the state has now become a thriving job market for workers from other regions of the country, the official agencies were finding it difficult to keep track of these silent and unfamiliar implications.

8. Intrastate Migration

8.1. Another trend of migration, different from the above-mentioned trends, was observed recently according to which "while migration continues to be a significant factor in the growth of these metropolitan regions, it is still not a predominant trend. Further, much of this migration is from within the state and not from other states."[34] Accordingly, a study revealed that only 15.00 per cent of educated migrants are attracted to Mumbai, where interstate migration is more than intra state, in all other metropolises intrastate migration was the principal component of the migrant quantum. It revealed that Mumbai had 61.00 to 63.00 per cent interstate migrants, the number of intrastate migrants remained between 36.00 to 37.00 per cent between 2001 and 2008.[35] The study further revealed migrants from within the state preferred to live in satellite townships like Thane and Navi Mumbai.

9. Domestic Migrant Labour in Kerala

A recent Study in Kerala about implications of serious social problems as a result of the stay of migrant labourers in that state revealed that there were over 25 Lakh [i.e., 7-8 per cent of the states population migrant labourers are there and around 2,35,000 new domestic migrants arrive there every year.[36] This study, conducted by Gulati Institute of Finance and Taxation for State Labour and Rehabilitation Department observed the situation as is mentioned below:

[i] Over 75.00 per cent of this domestic migrant labour belongs to five states of West Bengal, Bihar, Assam, U.P. and Odisha. Majority of these labourers belong to the age group of 18 to 30 years, which has effected the age group composition in the state. On an average, every labourer sends home at least Rs 70,000 annually. Together they send Rs 17,500 crore to their homes every year.

[ii] The migration of domestic labour within the country has created difficulty for governments to keep track of even though such relocation of people seeking better life conditions leads significant economic and social changes, especially in the destination state/ states.

[iii] The domestic migrant labourers have started entering all skills and sectors existing in the state. All occupations related to manufacturing, hotel and restaurants, trade and agriculture sectors have become heavily dependent on migrant labour.

[iv] While earlier migrants were seeking manual jobs and unskilled work in construction and employment sectors in and around cities and towns, the present domestic migrant labour was spread over both rural and urban areas and has percolated into all professions in Kerala.

[v] The major draw for these migrants are:

  [a] the rapid urbanisation and expansion of urban informal sector in Kerala,

  [b] the opening up of opportunities as a result of the international migration, especially to the Gulf countries, of the local people,

  [c] the relunctance of the educated unemployed youth in the state to do what they consider as 'menial jobs',

[d] the drastic fall in the levels of fertility that has caused a decline in the young working-age population, and

[e] the comparatively higher wage structure in the state.[37]

[vi] The migrant laboureres have not only outnumbered the local workers in many professions but have also totally replaced them, not just in manual jobs but in the manufacturing sector and in some specific services and professions.

[vii] Domestic migrant labour has a very visible and considerable presence even in the small towns of Kerala. So, as their population grow sand as they stayon in the state, these migrant communities will tend to assert their identity and rights, which in turn could lead to antagonism and tension with the local population.

[viii] Migrant labourers tend to live together in crowded tenements that often lack basic facilities and give rise to complaints from the local people about lack of hygiene and pollution of water sources. Most of them left their homes in teens and worked in several other Indian states before their arrival in Kerala.

[ix] One of the immediate issues such as large population, particularly male and young, raises was that lack of opportunities of leisure and their emotional-sexual needs . Parks, city centres, gardens and open spaces are the only spots where they meet and interact with relatives and friends. But, even these spots are very few in Kerala and their presence on these spots irritate the locals. In this situation, prostitution stands rampant among the migrant labourers which is carried out under veils of secrecy.[38]

References

1. "Behind the Exodus", *Frontline*, Chennai, September 21, 2012, p. 5.
2. See NSS report, quoted in *Frontline*, *Ibid.*
3. *Ibid.*
4. *Ibid.* "The New Reality".
5. *Ibid.*
6. *Ibid.*
7. *Ibid.*
8. *Ibid.*
9. *Ibid*, No. 1.
10. *Ibid.*

11. *Ibid.*
12. *Ibid.*
12A. *Ibid.*
13. *Ibid.*
14. *Ibid.*
14A. *Ibid.*
15. "Push Factors", *Ibid*, p.12.
16. "Social Leveller", *Ibid.*, pp.15-16.
17. *Ibid.*
18. *Ibid.*
19. *Ibid.*
20. *Ibid.* p. 16.
21. Report on "Labour Migration in Kashmir" by Dr B.A. Dabla [J&K, 2013].
22. *Ibid.*
23. *Ibid.*
24. "Desperate Migration", No. 1, p.18.
25. "History of Hostility", No. 1, pp. 23-25.
26. *Ibid.*
27. Seen as a Problem", No. 1, pp. 30-31..
28. "Replacement Migration", No. 1, pp. 28-30.
29. *Ibid.*
30. *Ibid.*
31. *Ibid.*
32. *Ibid.*
33. *Ibid.*
34. Reported in *The Times of India*, New Delhi, February 6, 2013.
35. *Ibid.*
36. See "The Other HALF" BY R. Krishnakumar, *Frontline* [Chennai], March 22, 2013.
37. *Ibid.*
38. *Ibid.*

4

The Kashmiri Pandit Migration of 1990-1991: A Sociological Study

1. Introduction

[i] The concept of migration essentially refers to the movement of human beings from one place of residence to another place of residence temporarily or permanently. The Oxford Dictionary of Sociology explains it in terms of permanent movement of individuals and groups across political boundaries in to new residential areas and communities. This process has been experienced at the global, regional and national level simultaneously. Sociologically, migration is characterised with four main features. First, it involves the constant movement from one place of residence to another place of residence over a period of time with certain reason to do so. Second, it includes debasement of one unit of residence at one place and subsequent establishment of another unit of residence at other place. Third, the process emerges as the social phenomenon as it engulfs the entire social life, especially attitudes and behaviour. Fourth, while many factors of involuntary nature trigger the process of national/international migration, its voluntary type has proved more effective, productive and stable in terms of implications.

[ii] Similarly, migration has set implications on the migrant as well as host society. First, migration generally creates demographic change in host societies which reflects in their population composition and fertility-mortality rates. Second, migration gives rise to the plurality of cultures, religions, languages and ethnicity in the host societies. Third, the emergence of plurality is followed by problems of competition, control and conflict and so on. Fourth, mass migration paves the way for giving rise to new cultures and civilisations.

2. Past Migration in Kashmir

[i] Like other societies in the world, the Kashmiri society too has undergone the process of migration with far reaching consequences for its inhabitants. In the ancient times, people of different origins and races came to Kashmir and many of them settled here. In the medieval times also, Kashmir experienced processes of in-migration and out-migration. In the former case, many aliens, especially Mughals, Afghans, Sikhs and Dogras, came as rulers and some of them settled here. In the same period, thousands of missionaries came to Kashmir from Central Asia and many of them, after converting locals to Islam, settled here. In the latter case, thousands of locals were compelled to migrate outside Kashmir to different parts of northern and central India. Pandit Jawaharlal Nehru and Sir Mohammad Iqbal represent those migrant communities from Kashmir.

3. Migration in Contemporary Times

[i] The Kashmiri society experienced the processes of in and out migration more significantly in modern times. In the first case, some tiny groups such as professionals, technocrats, experts, bureaucrats-administrators and businessmen came here and settled subsequently. In the second case, out-migration started from early decades of 20th century and that was intensified after 1947. This may explain the trend of out-migration among the KPs to different cities of post-independent India for educational and economic factoRs The rationale of this argument lies in the fact that KPs generally composed a near-total literate community. So, its members usually wanted to get higher technical, professional and most modern qualifications not only in the state of J&K but in the whole country. This trend of migration could not be avoided in that situation. Moreover, this trend of migration intensified partly because the highest qualification and merit of the KPs could not be adjusted in the state and partly because their conventional proportion in government jobs got decreased consistently in post-1947 decades in the state. The local talent of other communities in the state got adjusted in the state. This case of out-migration by KPs has certain parallel examples in the post-independent India such as the case of Tamil Brahmins.

4. 1989 KP Migration

[i] Kashmir experienced a radical type of mass migration in 1989-1992 in which period near-total members of the KP community migrated to Jammu and other cities and towns in India. The migration was so fast that, within a few years time, the entire residential colonies, mohallas,

and villages of KPs became deserted completely. They could not take any moveable property items with them. Even they left their domestic and daily-use items which could not be taken. It was because they were given the impression that they will return immediately after the rebellion in Kashmir will be crushed and finished.

[ii] Though this mass migration proved devastating for the community and its future, its causation has been extremely politicised. While some put the entire blame on the militants, especially "guest" militants, others held the then state government and its machinery responsible completely for this unprecedented exodus. In reality, the mass migration at that time was triggered by political and militant environment. It follows that, militancy conditions created due to the presence of foreign militants, the KPs felt a collective threat in which they felt compelled to leave Kashmir immediately and even leaving behind their entire moveable and immoveable property. The then government did nothing to stop this mass migration, rather it was not capable of that strength at that time. Thus this mass migration was a collective/community decision in which about 90 - 95 per cent of its members left Kashmir in early 1990s.

[iii] After KP community migrated to Jammu and other city, they were exposed to a pathetic situation which gave a shock to most, especially senior, membeRs They had to live in sub-human conditions in migrant camps made of cloth-based material in very hot, harsh and adverse weather conditions. While there seems some scope for disagreement about the causation of mass migration, but there seems no disagreement in the proposition about its devastating and dangerous effect on the entire community. Every individual, especially women, elder and children, in each family and group in the community had to face acute problems and their future as a distinctive community seemed a distant reality.

5. Methodology of the Study

[i] In the background of highly undesirable conditions in the KP migrant camps in Jammu, the author developed the idea of studying the crucial impact of migration with special reference to its implications on attitudes, behaviour and problems. This study was carried out in 2004-2005 within sociological and empirical framework. It was sponsored by University Grants Commission, New Delhi. The field work for this study was carried out in four migrant camps of Purkhu, Muthi, Mushriwallan and Nagrotta. Three visits during 2004-2005 were made to these camps by chief investigator and research investigator. A detailed

questionnaire was formulated and, within its framework, interviews were held in the migrant camps with one or more than one members of the family. The participant observation method was also used to get actual and real information, ideas and views of the respondents who were actually living in different camps. They belonged to different sexes, age groups, literacy groups, rural-urban areas and economic background.

6. **Findings of the Study**

[i] *Nature, time and number:* The migration of KPs 1989 started from and it was of the community type. After taking a collective decision in most compelling situation, they migrated at mass level in the mohalla and village groups. While dominant majority of migrants got immediate accommodation in to the make-shift migrant camps, some of them got shelter with their relatives and friends. Again, majority of them left all moveable and immoveable property in Kashmir, minority of them took some domestic items with them. As per the estimates of the study, the KP migrants got accommodated in the following places:

(a) migrant camps arranged by the government 62.00 per cent
(b) close relatives 14.00 per cent
(c) self-owned houses 10.00 per cent
(d) rented houses, flats and rooms 11.00 per cent
(e) friends, etc. 03.00 per cent

[ii] *Phases of migration:* It was observed that while the migration from Kashmir started in 1989, it reached to its climax in early 1990s. It may be argued that this migration was undertaken in three inter-related phases. The first phase started in 1989 with mass migration by entire families, mohallas and villages. This mass-level migration was triggered by the presence of foreign militants in the valley and killing of some Pandit personalities. The phase, also characterised by mass migration of entire families, was experienced in early 1990s when the state government failed to stop the killing spree by militants. This migration was undertaken in the darkness of night [in order to avoid the reaction of the majority community in Kashmir] and with complete support of the government administration. The third phase of migration started from mid-1990s and was comparatively less crowded. The KPs in this phase had stayed in Kashmir till the last moment for protecting their property, especially in the rural areas. But, when the situation deteriorated in Kashmir and they became target of the militants and uniformed gun holders, they felt no alternative

except to migrate. In this way, about 90 per cent of the KPs living in Kashmir migrated from Kashmir.

[iii] *Number of KP migrants:* There are not exact figures available about the number of migrants who migrated during three phases because no census or survey or any other documentation was carried out in this regard. But, this information was revealed, in response to a specific question about number of migrants from Kashmir and living in different states in India, in the Rajya Sabha in July 2003 by the union government. The details of this information follows:

-	Total number of migrant households	56,246 hh.	2,81,230 mem.
-	No. of migrant households at Jammu	34,305 hh.	1,71,525 mem.
-	No. of migrant households at Delhi	19,338 hh.	96,690 mem.
-	No. of migrant household. Other places in India	2,603 hh.	13,015 mem.
-	No. of mig. Nh. Living in camps in Jammu	4,778 hh.	23,890 mem.

[iv] *Composition of migrants:* It seems important to note that the migrants from Kashmir, particularly in the second and third phases, composed of KPs and migrants from other communities too, though their proportion was very less. As per the information released by J&K government in 2003, the composition of registered migrants was as mentioned below:

-	Kashmiri Pandits	33,000 hh.	1,65,000 mem.
-	Kashmiri Muslims	1,600 hh.	8,000 mem.
-	Kashmiri Sikhs	1,656 hh.	8,280 mem.

[v] *Accommodation and environment:* After the migration from Kashmir to Jammu, the KP migrants had the accommodation which was neither satisfactory nor desirable. While minority of the migrants lived in self constructed houses, J&K government flats and rented flats and rooms, majority of them lived in migrant camps or rented rooms. The condition of accommodation in the latter case can be characterised as pathetic and miserable. The living conditions in the camps were worst. A family had a single room accommodation which was bed-room cum drawing-room cum sitting-room cum study room. There was no proper sanitation, water-electricity supply and the environment was very dirty and stinking.

The harsh weather conditions had more adverse effects on the health of women, children and elderly.

[vi] *Demographic Impact:* Immediately after migrating from Kashmir, the demographic impact was felt by the sensitive section of the KP community. This impact may be explained in terms of disturbing mortality-fertility trends, abnormal sex behaviour, disturbed reproductive health, and so on. The change in the marriage pattern from endogamous to exogenous had also effected the entire productive behaviour pattern. More important effect was that there was no official record or census of these migrants within or outside the state. This will certainly effect the future of the community. In addition, their demographic features could not be registered separately as is usually done in case of every different community.

[vii] *Loss of Property:* As has been mentioned earlier, near total KP migrants could not take with them the moveable property and had to leave behind the immoveable property too without any custody. It was estimated that even 20 per cent of them could not take with them domestic and daily use items. Some of them disposed of some property items at very cheap cost. It was observed that, after KPs left the valley, many hoodlums and thieves looted these unoccupied houses and, later on, security forces were also found involved in this loot and plunder. The migrants who migrated in second and third phases got some time to dispose off their property at very cheap prices. According to an estimate in 2004, the following percentage of property of KPs was sold legally through local agents:

- 1989 - 1992 14.00 houses 07.00 land
- 1993 - 1999 28.00 houses 20.00 land
- 2000 - 2004 36.00 houses 28.00 land

It was in this background that the state government had to impose ban on these property dealings through formal legislation.

[viii] *Educational loss for Rural Migrants:* The rural migrants migrated after their counterparts did it earlier. But, as they remained backward in Kashmir, they maintained the same status in Jammu. This happened particularly in education and economic fields. While urban Pandits were ahead of their rural counterparts, this pattern and difference intensified in Jammu. Thus while rural boys and girls could not pursue higher professional and technical education and could not increase economic status and economic opportunities, the urban boys and girls were able to materialise all these benefits and opportunities.

[ix] *Deteriorating Health:* It was generally observed that the health of the KP migrants, especially of the elder generation, deteriorated extremely. They had to face the rise of certain dreaded diseases which needed serious and specialised treatment. The hot weather conditions created further complexities for the health of KP migrants of all age groups. It was estimated at that time that the following diseases had risen among KP migrants in the following intensity:

- Cardiac/heart related diseases	30 - 45 per cent
- Neurological diseases	25 - 35 per cent
- Hypertension and related diseases	40 - 60 per cent
- Blood pressure and related diseases	45 - 65 per cent
- Depression and other psychological diseases	47 - 65 per cent
- Other physical and mental diseases	30 - 60 per cent

[x] *Life conditions in Migrant camps:* It was observed that the migrant camps were like 'urban slums' in which the KPs lived a miserable life in sub-human conditions. They had no sufficient basic facilities which included pure drinking water, electricity, proper living space, and health and environment facilities. No PHC was provided to the camps. Though all migrant camps fall within urban/municipal limits, not many urban facilities were offered to these camps. It was observed that there were common bath rooms and open latrines which made the inhabitants' life like a hell. At that time, the migrant families were paid a petty amount of Rs 1,800 per month for a family, which hardly fulfilled its basic needs. Even this amount was not paid in time and regularly. It was also reported that the migrant camps were exposed to various offences of the criminal elements.

The most important problem of KP migrants in camps was that the family had one room accommodation for all purposes. While it was unimaginable for many Pandits, it created many problems for them as individuals and members of family. There was total lack of privacy in the camps which gave rise to many psychological, social and cultural problems, especially for those who were recently married.

[xi] *Family and Marriage:* The dominant family unit among KPs, especially belonging to rural areas, was of joint type. But, after migration, it was

exposed to new challenges in the new environment outside Kashmir. So, it was observed that the structure and function of joint family started passing through transformation to it nuclear type. Second, the pattern and practices of marriage experienced a serious change in which the endogamous marriage was replaced by exogamous marriage. A brief and formal survey gave the picture which reflects in the following data:

Changed attitude of the KPs after migration about exogamous marriage

Response	*Male*	*Female*
Yes	84 - 90 per cent	60 - 70 per cent
No	16 - 33 per cent	28 - 48 per cent
Partly yes and partly no	64 - 80 per cent	34 - 42 per cent

Other important change observed was the change in the criteria of selection of the marriage partner. It was caste earlier but it was now extra-caste criteria such as education, economic status, accommodation and so on. It was in that context that the KPs opted for marriage with all communities having the pan-Indian character. At the same time, late marriage emerged as a phenomenon in the community. According to our estimate at that time, the average age of marriage among KP migrants was 28-30 years for males and 26-29 years for females. It was generally felt that there was dearth of qualified and eligible grooms within the community. Shortage of suitable boys was felt seriously by most of the families. So, they were in demand in marriage market and demanded huge dowry from girl's families.

[xii] *Culture and Language:* It was generally observed that it was not possible for KP migrants in Jammu and other cities in India to maintain completely the traditional culture, especially language, dress and food habits. They were conscious of this situation but could not stop this process of erosion because there was hardly any functional utility for traditional cultural practices in alien lands, particularly for the younger generation. In this situation, dropping of traditional cultural features seemed a natural response to the challenges and demands in the changed or newly-adopted life condition. However, some exceptions were found among elder members of the community but they hardly matter in the situation of great and radical transformation.

7. **Other Relevant Points**

The fact stands with statistical evidence that while dominant majority of Kashmiri Pandits [KPs] migrated en mass to different areas of India, especially Jammu, from 1990, minority of them didn't migrate and stayed in Kashmir during last two decades. As per government of India information, provided in Lok Sabha in July 2002, there was following number of migrant households and their members:

[i] total number of households 56,243

[ii] total members in these households 2,81,230

[see Dr B.A. Dabla, Sociological Implications of Pandit Migration in Kashmir, New Delhi, 2007].

On the other hand, as per the estimate of this author, there were 2000 - 2500 households [with 10,000 - 11,500 members] of KPs living in the Kashmir valley in 2006. While about 90 per cent of them lived in all colonies with neighbors, about 10 per cent [who were mainly govt. employees] lived in security zones/areas. [See Dr B.A. Dabla] According to the statement of K.P. Sangarsh Samiti, a socio-political organisation of KPs who stayed in the valley, there were 32,000 KPs in 1992 and 19,865 in 1998. According to his same statement, there are 3,440 KPs living in the valley at present. [See Kashmir Life, 10th October 2009]

Those KPs who stayed back in Kashmir suffered like their Muslim neighbouRs They had to face psychological, social, economic, cultural, religious and other problems but they didn't debase themselves from the Kashmir roots. They shared positives and negatives of life with their Muslim brothers and sisteRs They managed left-over Hindu temples and saved them from taking over by non-Kashmiri priests. They didn't sell their property and retained their material roots here. They faced acute cultural and marriage problems, but preferred to stay in the Kashmiri cultural ethos. In this context, who can forget the personalities of Professor C.L. Veshin and Professor M.L. Lidoo.

In recent months, serious negotiations have started about the mass return of KPs to Kashmir. Serious efforts are on to develop a broader framework and to draw a plan in this regard. The J&K government has recently announced a rehabilitation and financial package amounting to about Rs. 16,000 crores in the initial stage. As per this package, any family willing to return will be accommodated by the govt. till they construct their own houses, for which Rs. 7.50 lakh will be provided to each family. Those who wish to establish income generating units would be entitled to cash assistance of Rs. 5 lakh [2.50 lakh as subsidy and 2.50 lakh as loan]. Finally, school-going children of KPs will be entitled to a monthly stipend of Rs. 750 each. [see details Greater Kashmir, 30.9.2009]

Since this development is pleasing, it must be appreciated by all friends of Kashmir. But, at this stage, one should remain conscious of some existing facts. First, KPs will land in a place which stands radically different in comparison to earlier society and irreversible social transformation has occurred in it. Second, a new generation of children among KPs as well as KMs has emerged whose interaction has to be directed in proper and desirable perspective. Third, desirable and decent limits must be recognised and established regarding future economic and social competition. Fourth, the role of eminent and credible social notables like those of Bhajan Sopori and Sushil Razdan must be established and legitimised.

At this stage of implementation of govt. proposed rehabilitation package, the KPs who stayed in Kashmir throughout and faced various problems must not be ignored. They should be helped preferably in the following ways:

[a] They must be equally compensated, especially in establishing business and income generating units by providing loans and subsidies;

[b] The unemployed youth of this leftover community must get sufficient number of govt. jobs among the total number of jobs to be provided to KP;

[c] They must be provided monetary support for purchase of land and construction of houses; and

[d] They should be accepted as social and cultural 'mediators' between KMs and migrated KPs in the prevailing situation.

8. Concluding Points

[i] The observations which were made in 2004-05 were presented in the findings in previous sections. [For detailed findings see author's book entitled Sociological Implications of Pandit Migration in Jammu and Kashmir, Srinagar, 2008, J K Books] Primarily, the human and emotional concern with the plight of KP migrants life contributed to the initiation of academic study which was carried out with scientific and sociological orientation. Its real objective was to identify, analyse and highlight the extreme plight of life conditions in which majority of them were trapped and were compelled to live the life of an urban slum, which shocked anybody having human heart and human concern.

[ii] We feel that this sincere academic effort proved purposeful mainly because it succeeded in portraying the pathetic situation prevailing in migrant camps rationally and realistically. In reality, this academic and professional exercise represented one of the first attempts on the part of local experts-academics to make an objective study of KP migrants life which developed after their mass migration and gave rise to various crucial problems. It must be noted here that there was frank appreciation of this serious effort on the part of liberal and sincere representatives of the KP community. We value this gesture and this is our real social and cultural wealth.

[iii] The fact stands that there emerged some more important problems and issues which emerged in the post-2005 period. These include problems related to culture, language, political participation, identity, ideology and social interaction with other communities, and issues like return of KPs to Kashmir and J&K government's policy towards KPs rehabilitation. But, these problems and issues fall outside the scope of this paper. I am writing a separate paper on that theme.

5

Labour Migration in Kashmir: Sociological Findings

1. Introduction

[i] At the national level, the rural to urban migration emerged as the dominant trend in population movement from one place of residence to other place of residence. Consequently, millions of rural people migrated to urban areas in order to pursue economic objectives. In the existing situation of change, the rural sector could not incorporate the extra manual labour, mainly unskilled. So, they were compelled to move from their rural areas to urban areas where they could be adjusted in expanding urban and increasing industrial sectoRs

[ii] At the same time, at the national level, another parallel trend of migration was observed with considerable number of people from one state or many states to another state or states in the country. These people mainly belonging to the states where there were lesser economic resources and opportunities migrated to the states where they could be recruited temporarily or permanently in different economic sectoRs This demographic process proved a 'pan-Indian process' in the previous decades. In a recent report about this trend of migration in the state of Bihar, it was observed that, according to 2001 census reports, about 1.7 million people migrated from Bihar to other states in the country in the last one decade. [See Frontline, Chennai, September 21, 2012, p. 15] In another survey of the Bihari migrants' destination, carried out by Institute of Economic Studies, Patna, it was revealed that these people migrated to Panjab [up to 26.36 per cent of the total], Delhi [up to 21.34 per cent of the total], Maharastra [up to 15.06 per cent of the total], Haryana [up to 11.72 per cent of the total], and West Bengal [up to 05.86 per cent of the total]. [See *Ibid.*] However, the J&K state was not mentioned in this study, where migrant labourers [MLs] have migrated in large numbers in last three decades.

[iii] Regarding the social causation of this type of migration from Bihar, it was observed that "economic distress and caste exploitation" were also the reasons that "drove the poor villagers to migrate." These factors have also "made the backward class populations of Bihar the largest group of migrant workforce in India." [See *Ibid.*, p. 14]

[iv] In this broader context, millions of people leave their states of origin and arrive in the states of residence such as from Bihar to other states in India and from Panjab to other neighbouring states. The sole motive of this type of migration stands economic, i.e., the migrants intend to earn more amount of money than they earn at their places of origin in lieu of their work and services. These migrants included skilled, technical-profession trained and unskilled petty labour. In this national level pattern, the migrants from different states of India, especially Bihar, Panjab, U.P., Rajasthan, West Bengal, Haryana and other states, arrived here in Kashmir, stayed here in rural and urban areas, worked in sectors of economy and earned good money. In this process of migration, both migrant and host communities came into contact, interacted and effected each other.

[v] This process of migration of skilled and unskilled labour in J&K started from early 1970s , though some individual migrants had landed here even before 1970s. This process expanded and progressed and reached to its heights by late 1980s and 1990s. After the climax of migrant labour in J&K mid-1990s, this trend had gone down heavily with the initiation of militancy in J&K. But, after the militancy was controlled in the first decade of this century, this trend got revived and lakhs of labourers arrived in J&K again. Now, we have a strong migrant labour community present in J&K working in all sectors of economy and sending the money to their homes back in different states of India. The rise and fall of the migrant labour in J&K can be seen in the following diagram:

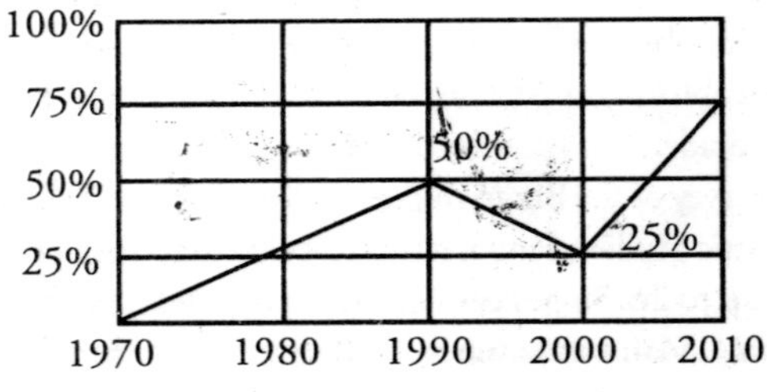

Rise and fall in the Migrant Labour J&K

[vi] In the above context, this sociological study was carried out in the Kashmir province of J&K state during 2009-2010. The Principal Investigator of this empirical study was Bashir Ahmad Dabla, Head, Department of Sociology, University of Kashmir, Srinagar. While the supervisor of this field study was Sofia Hassan, Department of Sociology, the research investigation was carried out by students of M. A. [final] Sociology belonging to the 2008-2009 batch. The list of these students has been attached at the end of this report. A brief report of the findings of this study was published in Journal of Society in Kashmir [official journal of the Department of Sociology], Vol. 2, No. 2, 2012.

Bashir Ahmad Dabla
Head, Department of Sociology,
University of Kashmir, Srinagar.

23 January 2013.
Srinagar, J&K.

Chapter II

1. Methodology

[i] *Empirical Orientation:* This study was carried out in the empirical framework. There was no theoretical or ideological bias involved in their application. So, it was aimed at arriving at conclusion/s only through empirical methodological tools and methods.

[ii] *Universe of the Study:* The universe of this study was composed of the Kashmir province in the state of J&K. It had ten administrative districts in which the outside migrant labour was present and their presence was felt in all districts which are:

[a] Srinagar	[b] Anantnag	[c] Baramulla
[d] Budgam	[e] Ganderbal	[f] Pulwama
[g] Shopian	[h] Kupwara	[i] Bandipora
[j] Kulgam.		

[iii] *Methods and Techniques of Research:* The following methods/techniques were utilised for carrying out this empirical study and reaching to some particular conclusions:

- *Questionnaire:* A detailed questionnaire was formulated and used by the researchers individually. It was a detailed questionnaire having various thematic questions [of open-ended and fixed-choice nature, depending upon the nature and demand of the concerned questions]. It was based on stratified and theme-oriented questions.

- *Interviews:* Generally, the questionnaires were filled by the trained researcheRs In some cases, there emerged the need for direct interviews in order to get clear, specific and relevant response. In that situation, the researchers adopted/used the interview technique and filled the information themselves or recorded it. This technique provided totality of the responses and complete information about various themes and questions under investigation.
- *Observation:* In some cases, the observation method proved more suitable, productive and relevant for getting the actual information/response. So, it was adopted in selective situations and selective cases. Most of the time, this observation was of "participant type" and, in this process, the researchers secured the response of the respondents after developing sufficient rapport with them and trust feeling between respondents and researcheRs In this way, the possibility of fake or wrong response was reduced considerably.
- *Training to Researchers:* Before going to the field for investigation, the researchers were trained in posing questions, recording their answers/responses, complexities and problems in conducting interviews and in making observation, particular the participant observation.

[iv] *Fieldwork*

[a] *Pilot Study:* Before carrying out the whole fieldwork, a pilot study was carried out among 20 per cent of total number of sample of respondents. It was meant to test the authenticity, suitability and relevance of the questionnaire and other methods-techniques to be adopted in this research. Finally, the results of the pilot study led to some revisions and changes in the first draft of the questionnaire.

[b] *Data Collection:* In the proper field work, the data collection was done by trained researchers through questionnaire, interview and participant observation. Moreover, descriptive information was also gathered from the field.

[c] *Trained Researchers:* As has been mentioned, the entire fieldwork was carried out by M.A. final students of Sociology of Kashmir University who were trained in detail in methodological tools, techniques, approaches and other aspects before sending them in the field. They were 40 in number and carried out this field investigation personally during the period of three months in the year 2009-2010.

[v] *Sample of the Study:* The sample of the study was sociological and representative . It gave representation to every sociological variable. The details follow:

[a] *Universe of the sample:* The universe of this sample was all 10 districts of the Kashmir region in J&K state. These districts have been mentioned in the previous section. [see section no. ii]

[b] *Number of Sample Respondents:* The total number of sample of respondents of this study was 4,200 belonging to all 10 districts in different proportions. Their proportion was follows:

Table 2.1 Total Number of Respondents in the Study

S.No.	*District*	*Number of respondents*	*S.No.*	*District*	*Number of respondents*
1.	Srinagar	440	6.	Kupwara	400
2.	Anantnag	440	7.	Pulwama	400
3.	Baramulla	440	8.	Kulgam	400
4.	Budgam	440	9.	Ganderbal	400
5.	Bandipora	400	10.	Shopian	400
				Total	4,200

Every district was given representation at the level of tehsils and blocks in order to make it more representative at all levels and in all fields.

[c] *Age Groups of the Sample*: The respondents in the sample of this study composed of the following age groups:

Table 2.2. Age Groups of Respondents of the Sample

S.No.	*Age Group*	*Number*	*Percentage*
1.	08 - 18 years	748	17.82
2.	19 - 30 years	2349	55.92
3.	31 - 45 years	867	20.64
4.	46 + years	236	05.61
5.	No response	000	00.00
	Total	4,200	100.00

[d] *Sex Composition:* The sample respondents had the following sex composition:

Table 2. 3. Sex Composition of the Sample

S.No.	*Sex*	*Number*	*Percentage*
1.	Males	3354	79.85
2.	Females	846	20.13
	Total	4,200	100.00

[e] *Marital Status:* The respondents in this study had the marital status as mentioned below:

Table 2. 4. Marital Status of the Respondents

S.No.	*Marital Status*	*Number*	*Percentage*
1.	Married	2425	57.73
2.	Not Married	1836	43.00
3.	Divorcee/separat/disput	61	01.45
	Total	4200	100.00

[f] *Income Status:* The respondents of this study belonged to different income groups as mentioned below:

Table 2. 5. Different Income Groups of the Respondents

S.No.	*Income group [per month]*	*Number*	*Percentage*
1.	Below Rs 5,000/-	1862	34.00
2.	5001 - 10000	1955	55.00
3.	10001 - 15000	301	07.16
4.	15001 - 20000	66	01.57
5.	20001 +	16	00.38
	Total	4200	100.00

[g] *Literacy Status:* The respondents of this study had the following literacy status:

Table 2. 6. Literacy Status of the Respondents

S.No.	*Literacy Status*	*Number*	*Percentage*
1.	Literate	1775	27.00
2.	Illiterate	2325	63.00
3.	Semi-literate	1000	10.00
	Total	4200	100.00

[h] *Language Status:* The respondents of this study had the following language status:

Table 2. 7. Language Status of the Respondents

S.No.	*Languages spoken/used*	*Number*	*Percentage*
1.	Hindi	1574	37.47
2.	Maithali	188	04.47
3.	Bhojpuri	565	13.45
4.	Gujarati	73	01.73
5.	Bengali	162	03.85
6.	Rajasthani	124	02.95
7.	Panjabi	219	05.21
8.	Urdu	411	09.78
9.	Nepali	08	00.19
10.	Kashmiri	17	00.40
11.	Bihari	474	11.20
12.	Any other	421	10.02
	Total	4200	100.00

[i] *Data Collection:* The trained investigators carried out the field investigation and collected all necessary data in all districts in a period of about three months.

[j] *Aggregation, Tabulation and Analysis:* After completing data collection, it was aggregated and tabulated according to the objectives and themes of this study. This manual process led us to the stage of explanation/analysis

of the data and reach at the proper, logical and scientific propositions and conclusions about all topics of this study.

[k] *Final Report:* After going through all such methodological and sociological stages of this empirical investigation, we were able to finalise the report of the study. Thus we were able to present the final report of this study.

Chapter III

Findings of the Study

1. Places of Origin of the Migrant Labour

1.1. The migrant labourers in the valley belonged to different places/states of India, especially from Northern, Southern and Central India. In the initial stage, these labourers came mainly from Bihar, the place of potential source of migration. Subsequently, the labourers from other places/states were informed about this situation in Kashmir and were sufficiently motivated by the Bihari labourers . After some time, they too migrated to Kashmir. Our inquiry about the origin of places of residence of the migrant labour revealed as has been shown in the following table:

Table 3. 1. Places of Origin of the Migrant Labour

S.No.	*Migrants state/ place of origin*	*Number*	*Percentage*
1.	Bihar	1971	46.93
2.	Uttar Pradesh	644	15.33
3.	Gujarat	361	08.86
4.	Rajasthan	360	08.80
5.	West Bengal	342	08.14
6.	Punjab	145	03.45
7.	Madhya Pradesh	78	01.86
8.	Nepal	35	00.83
9.	Jharkhand	13	00.31
10.	Other states in India	575	13.69
	Total	4200	100.00

1.2. The table above reveals that a dominant group of migrant labourers have their origin in the state of Bihar. Their proportion to the total migrant labour force in Kashmir was 46.93 per cent and their dominance among the migrants was revealed in all cities, towns and villages. There seem two determining reasons for their dominance, push and pull factoRs The push factor was related to the extreme poverty situation in Bihar, especially among the people belonging to Muslim minority community, while the pull factor pointed to the relative affluent economic situation in the state of J&K, especially in the Kashmir region. In the case of latter, i.e., the pull factor, the affluence does not refer to absolute and ideal type of affluence, but the economic conditions which enabled the locals to leave or shun their traditional occupations and adopt new occupations for themselves. These labourers from Bihar, popularly designated as the Bihari labour [BL] belonged to rural as well as to urban areas, share the similar culture, language and life style despite differences in religion, caste and language. They may be different from each other at many times and places, but they posed and presented themselves as a cohesive group in which they shared unique ideology, worldview and culture. This they adopt outside the state of Bihar during their period of migration but stand hardly concerned about this identity inside Bihar.

1.3. The second dominant group of migrant labour present in Kashmir was from the state of Uttar Pradesh [U.P.] which constituted 15.33 per cent of the total migrant labour force. This significant group of migrants was not so integrated and cohesive in comparison to the BL. They represented a dissimilar than a similar lot of culture as reveals in the state of U.P. While their attitudes differed within and without, their behaviour patterns also differed. For example, while labourers from Bihar usually used locally produced alcohol, thera, chuna, bidis and drugs, the labourers from U.P. did not usually involved themselves in alcohol consumption and drug behaviour. They belonged to different places and regions and spoke different languages-dialects. Their psychological bent of mind, social attitudes and work culture are entirely different, especially from the BL. They think differently, work differently and interact with locals differently. Though they belong to different religions, it does not lead to any conflict among them. However, they are less conscious and lesser assertive about their identity than the BL. Some of the locals prefer UPites to other migrant labourers [ML] for the former's politeness, patience, hard work, quality work, less problematic, lesser complex attitudes and work ethic.

1.4. The other significant group of Gujarat belongs to the Indian state of ML. It composed 08.86 per cent of the total ML in Kashmir. These labourers have started coming to Kashmir from early decades of the post-independence era. They usually came to work on some particular and specialised fields such as jewellary work, glass work and so on. The main feature of their migration to Kashmir was its continuity in comparison to ML from Bihar, U. P. and other states. It follows that ML from Bihar and U.P. may not continue to move to Kashmir every year necessarily. But, in the case of Gujarati labourers, they have been coming here regularly and without any long break and they intend to continue this tradition. They have been found less conscious and lesser assertive in the case of their distinctive identity. Through their social and cultural practices, they have conveyed the 'Gujarati homogeniety' in public, which was not resented by the locals. Comparatively, they have been found hard working, peaceful, and serious care-takeRs

1.5. Another group of significant presence and proportion of 08.60 per cent of the total Rajasthan belonged to the state of ML. These labourers maintained distinct social and cultural traits, spoke different languages-dialects and practised various cultural practices and rituals. In terms of psychological make-up and personality traits, they represent a different type from Bihar, U.P. and Gujarat. They were found highly tolerant, submissive, hard working, following work seriously, believing in work ethic and not violating occupational norms. They used to get lesser wages comparatively but they didn't involve in bargaining. Religious, regional and linguistic differences didn't make them socially segregative. They were non-violent in general attitudes and behaviour, especially in comparison to the BL. In terms of occupational skills, they maintained certain basic standards. Some of them were exceptionally good in their areas of specialisation. They also lived a simple life comparatively and sent most of their earned income to their homes back through official and legal sources. They were very less involved in hawala-type transactions.

1.6. The next group of the West Bengal belonged to the state of ML. In fact, the Bengali labourers [BL] started arriving in Kashmir in smaller groups long back and have now accumulated the strength of 8.14 per cent of the total ML in Kashmir at present. They generally represented the culture of hard work and that also with commitment. Though most of them belonged to a different religion that of the locals, their religiosity never reflected or effected their life and relations with the host community. In reality, they represented mutually adjustable and amicable social ethos. Secularism was the supreme value and ideal to which they attached a lot of importance. In practice, they proved sincere and committed workeRs So, their hosts and employers generally liked them.

They belonged to certain particular occupational fields in which they have developed exclusive specialisation. So, they were always in demand in Kashmir. Some of them were staying here for the whole year, including the severe winter months of December, January and February, which is not the case with most of the ML groups in Kashmir. The relationship of the BL with the host community stands cordial to excellent. They have close and intense relationship with the local families. In this context, some of the local families have married their boys or girls with the Bangali migrant matches. These Bengali boys had higher status occupational jobs and maintained minimum economic standard which enabled them to present 'eligible and deserving grooms' to the concerned families.

These inter-marriage between Bangali and Kashmiri boys and girl have proved stable and so continued with lesser problems. This type of marriage stood completely different from inter-Bengali-Kashmiri marriages, in which intention of deceipt and fraud was involved. According to this type, the Kashmiri boys go to West Bengal and involve some innocent and ignorant Bengali girls and take them to Kashmir on the promise of proper marriage with them. After they arrive here, the earlier promise is not fulfilled in many cases. Some girls out of them are sold to other men here clinedestinly [who use and abuse them sexually forcefully] or are used for prostitution purposes. Only some lucky Bengali girls got real Kashmiri husbands. The local police has registered many such cases in the past decades and were also reported in the local print media.

1.7. Another significant component of the ML in Kashmir was represented by labourers from different areas of Panjab. These people compose 03.45 per cent of the total ML force. Most of them belong to the Sikh religion and practise fully the folk culture of their state. They were highly conscious about their identity and assert that identity always. They were usually skilful and specialised in certain particular occupations and charged higher rates for their expertise. Thus their expert skill gave them more income. So, they were in high demand in urban as well as in rural areas throughout the year. They were specially needed in the renovation and beautification of business establishments, especially shops in the markets.

During their work in Kashmir, the PLs have proved extremely hard working, innovativel, creativel and with devotion and commitment. They have developed highest degree of community sentiment and celebrate religious festively and other community occasions with enthusiasm. They organised the 'community kitchen' on every religious occasions in which more or less all members of the community participated, which created strong kind of religious solidarity among them in Kashmir. They were necessarily employed by their community members and others equally. They also participated in the community programmes in which the community poor people were taken full care.

1.8. The ML in Kashmir also composed of three minor groups whose origin can be traced to Madhya Pradesh [M.P.], Jharkhand [J&K] and Nepal, the neighbouring country. While the proportion of two former groups was 01.80 per cent and 00.31 per cent of the total ML, the latter had 00.83 per cent share in the total. While these workers were petty and unskilled labourers in the fields of construction, agriculture, tourism, horticulture and other sectors, the Nepalese workers were engaged exclusively in the security sector, where in they performed the role of security guards. They were popularly known by a name called 'Bahadur'. They were usually engaged by elite families for their members and property security. They were considered as the best possible security personnel available in India. They were also considered physically strong, mentally not corrupt, honest in dealings, morally upright, and always simple and humble.

1.9. Finally, 13.69 per cent of the total ML in Kashmir belonged to the rest of Indian states, especially in the South. These different migrant groups belonged to diverse occupations, specialised fields, different skills, crafts and arts and were working in as diverse fields as hotels to shops of gold ornaments to restaurants to roadside Dhabas.

1.10. Thus we are in a position to argue that a significant degree of migration to Kashmir took place in post-1947 period due to push and pull factoRs The number of the ML has increased [and decreased in between] tremendously in last four decades and their presence was felt seriously by the locals, especially in the long-term and short-term implications of this largest trend of migration. During their stay in Kashmir, these migrant groups and sub-groups maintained their national identity and their regional or sub-regional identities. So, they reveal the broader plurality and diversity of the pan-Indian society and allowed every group and sub-group to work in their respective field and earn positively certain amount of income in lieu of their work and services. All these features of their economic, social and cultural life contributed to the phenomenon characterised by national integration at the micro as well as macro level. The actions and interactions between the migrants and hosts created a sense of national identity and national concern. In brief, it has led to the ideas and ideals of nationhood.

2. Phases of Migration in Kashmir

2.1. In fact, the LM to Kashmir started after independence. As a result, the movement of smaller groups of migrants didn't show serious impact. But, from early 1970s, the arrival of migrants increased heavily. The major factors for this organised wave of migrants can be identified as follows:

[i] initiation of the IT revolution in the country and in the state of J&K;

[ii] intensification and acceleration in the processes of migration in the country, especially region to region and state to state trends; and

[iii] expanding processes of interaction and integration within the country and the people in J&K state.

The real period of LM started from 1970s. This long period of migration can broadly be divided [on the basis of the record of arrival of ML in the Kashmir valley] in three general phases;

[a]	First phase	1970 - 1990
[b]	Second phase	1991 - 2000
[c]	Third phase	2001 - 2010

In this connection, when we enquired from respondents of this study, their response revealed the figures and phases as mentioned in the following table:

Table 3. 2. Four Specific Phases of Labour Migration

S.No.	*Phase No.*	*Years involved*	*Number*	*Percentage*
1.	First phase	1970 - 1980	251	05.97
2.	Second phase	1980 - 1990	848	22.65
3.	Third phase	1990 - 2000	838	20.19
4.	Fourth phase	2000 - 2010	2150	51.19
	Total	1970 - 2010	4200	100.00

2.2. The first phase of 1970-1980 [as conveyed by 05.97 per cent of the respondents] migration was not highly significant comparatively as explained above. There was even less than usual migration experienced in Kashmir during this phase mainly because of political instability here. The real and potential trends of LM started from early 1980s and following years, in which there was huge rush of skilled and unskilled labourers, especially from Bihar and U.P. As was observed, this phase was characterised with features such as highest number of ML who arrived in Kashmir, highest wages for skilled, semi-skilled, unskilled and other labourers in all sectors and fields of local economy. These workers worked mainly in sectors such as construction, business, trade and commerce, agriculture, horticulture and tourism. This BL got solid amount of money from their work in Kashmir which they sent to their homes.

These labourers came first to the cities and then spread to towns and villages and their presence was felt in every area. They belonged to many states, in addition to Bihar, such as West Bengal, Panjab, Rajasthan and Madhya Pradesh. It was found that they were involved in cyclical type of migration. It meant that they were usually individuals without families and worked for the season. Afterwards, they left for home and came here again in the next working season. This circular migration was repeated every year.

2.3. The second phase of LM in Kashmir was identified as the period from 1980 - 1990 conveyed in the response of 22. 65 per cent of the respondents. It proved a mature period of migration in which relatively significant number of labourers arrived in Kashmir. In addition to performing the economic role, they tried to develop social, cultural and religious contact with the local community. While in the former case, i.e., economic role, they succeeded, but, in the latter case, they were not successful. This phase also proved highly intensive as well as extensive in terms of the ML presence. It was in that context that they tried to establish socio-cultural rapport with the host community. However, this trend of migration got lost with the emergence of militancy in J&K. In that particular situation, about half of the ML had to leave Kashmir in a year because of the threat of violence. On the other hand, less than half ML stayed here and did the normal economic activity. With the increase in militancy activities, in which MLs were also involved and threatened, many of them left for their states. Even then thousands of ML stayed and worked in Kashmir during the high militancy years also. It was reported in the press, some ML too joined the militancy movement and some of them got killed and injured. During this entire period, they remained aloof from the local community and did not establish any social rapport.

2.4. The third phase of LM, i.e., 1990 - 2000, was characterised with two parallel features. While the half decade of this period experienced backward trend in migration, the latter half of the period observed the opposite trend in the environment of decreasing militancy conditions. In the first half of this phase, there was strong presence of militancy and militants. Despite this abnormal condition, they carried out their daily work and earned sufficient amount, which was more than their needs. So, they were able to save money which they sent to their homes in different states. Thus they didn't face serious economic loss despite militancy. But, in terms of life style, culture and behaviour, they didn't mix with the local population and live an isolated and alienated social and cultural life. They could not adopt and maintain the local cultural traits.

2.5. But, in the second half of the decade, there was an opposite trend, i.e., heavy increase in the arrival of ML. It was mainly because the Indian security forces had broken the back of militancy and militants' presence was not visible as looked earlier. This time, the LM had other partners who belonged to many other states in the country. With the arrival of huge number of tourists in Kashmir, the number of LMs also increased, there were different and specialised and skilled labourers to fill the needs in the field. This time again, the LMs spread in all areas, in all sectors, and in all fields. They had better qualifications, techniques and so on. There was also heavy increase in the wages which benefitted the migrant labourers [MLs] absolutely. But, at the same time and like in the first half decade, there was not any significant change in the pattern of interaction between migrant and host communities. Both these communities lived separate social and cultural lives and any violation of that norm led to some disturbances also.

2.6. These three major phases of LM have been portrayed in the following diagram:

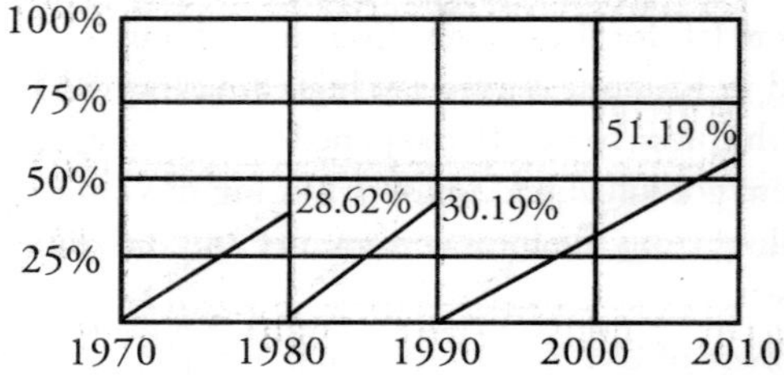

Three major phases of Labour Migration

3. **Whole-time or Part-time Stay of the ML in Kashmir**

3.1. Our research revealed that LMs came to Kashmir individually or with their families. While the first category of LMs was in majority, the second was in minority. The first category came generally in the first phase of migration, while the second category arrived in second and third phases of migration. The relevant investigation among the respondents revealed the following information about migrants:

[i]	Migrants as individuals	48.13 per cent	[1989/4200]
[ii]	Migrants with families	19.84 per cent	[834/4200]

It follows that majority of migrants had arrived in Kashmir as individuals, i.e., 48.13 per cent of the total MLs. Some of them called their families later on when they made accommodation and other arrangements here. On the other hand, minority of 19.84 per cent MLs arrived in Kashmir with their families. While most of the individual migrants were skilled, professional and technical workers, who fetched comparatively more wages, migrants with families were often unskilled and non-professional workers and earned comparatively lesser wages. They had to face many problems here in comparison to individual migrants. As a result of this situation, the individual migrants could earn and save more than their family counterparts. Consequently, the latter could sent more amount of money to their homes than the former. In fact, the migrant families remained tight economically throughout their stay and could save much amount of money. They also could not improve their living condition considerably.

3.2. The empirical research also revealed number of MLs stayed in Kashmir for different periods. While some stayed for the whole year/season, others worked here for the 'work season' only and left before the onset of winter. Their stay and work in Kashmir was determined by factors which included migrants' degree of physical resistance of cold weather conditions, need for amount of money, and their traditional nature and season of work cycle. The specific results of our investigation among respondents gave the concerned information mentioned below:

[i]	those who stayed for whole year	14.70 per cent	[621/4200]
[ii]	those who stayed for work season	45.52 per cent	[1912/4200]

It follows from the above table that a minority of 14.70 per cent of the total MLs stayed here for whole of the year, even in the harsh winter conditions in the valley. Now they have fully adopted to the extreme cold conditions. On the other hand, nearly half of the MLs, i.e., 45.52 per cent of the total, stayed and worked here for the season period only. It means that they worked here in the summer and autumn [from March to November] season. While some of them worked here for 8 -9 months, many them worked here for 6 - 8 months. It may also be inferred that individual migrants generally stayed here for longer period in comparison to family migrants who stayed for shorter periods. This aspect was also related to the occupational specialisation. It was because some occupations were in operation throughout the year, while others did operate for some months only.

4. Major Occupations of the MLs in Kashmir

4.1. As was expected, the ML belonged to all important occupations needed in the society. However, every society has given preference and attached priority for particular occupations. Since the Kashmiris were changing their occupations fast in the present times, these were systematically replaced by the MLs which came from outside the state. In this important process, while the local occupational manpower left their specialised arts and crafts, the ML immediately replaced these vacant positions. Our inquiry among the MLs about the occupational diversity gave the information noted in the following table:

Table 3.3. Major Occupations of the Migrant Labourers

S.No.	Name of Occupation	Number	Percentage
1.	Masons	730	17.40
2.	Carpenters	445	10.60
3.	Painters	324	07.71
4.	Hair-dressers	164	03.90
5.	Agricultural labourers	18	00.42
6.	Salesmen shops	63	01.50
7.	Skilled labourers	1002	23.85
8.	Cobblers	105	02.50
9.	Construction workers	10	00.23
10.	Tailors	40	00.95
11.	Ice-cream vendors	22	00.53
12.	Vegetable sellers	52	01.23
13.	Other occupations	924	22.00
14.	No response	300	07.14
	Total	4200	100.00

4.2. The above table reveals clearly that the occupational diversity existing in the ML was needed in the Kashmiri society. The largest category of MLs was composed of the unskilled labourers [whose percentage was 23.85 per cent of the total] who came in large numbers, especially from the states of Bihar and U.P., and worked in all sectors and fields of economy. Both men and women were involved in this labour force as it required no particular training or specific skills. It was also observed that children of these MLs were also engaged in the work. The wages of these labourers were always of some local standard or local criteria, which the MLs find 'satisfactory' and 'enough'. It was also because they could save and send some amount of money from these wages to their homes in addition to the amount which they spent on themselves. However, during the course of investigation, some cases of exploitation and manipulation on the part of elders and agents of MLs were noted.

4.3. The second category of MLs composed of misc. and common occupations which needed no particular training and experience. Their number was

924 out of 4,200, i.e., 22.00 per cent of the total. They got these jobs easily as there was less competition for these [jobs] and were benefitted economically in the lowest degree.

4.4 The third category of MLs composed of masons. It was in the context in which Kashmir experienced the wave for construction of residential houses in every area, rural and urban. This wave was so strong that thousands of masons and allied skilled and unskilled labourers got engaged in the important emerging sector. Though it represented an "unproductive sector", it started in early 1980s and still continues. The rise of this sector can be directly related to the prevailing status symbol of building a good residential house, which is also necessary due to harsh winter conditions. Thus the construction activity continued for the whole year and it gave more income benefits to the MLs and skilled personnel. It was observed that most of these technical and skilled personnel claiming of having some qualification and degrees were not correct. Some of them were even illiterate. But, they worked day and night, without any holiday and earned huge amount of money, some part of which they sent to their homes.

4.5 The following occupational category was of carpenters whose proportion was 10.60 per cent of thr total ML. Their conditions were more or less same as those of masons. They attracted higher wages in the local market and their professional in the field were paid highest wages in comparison to others of the same occupational status. They were in demand for the whole year and so were busy in off and on seasons. People waited for weeks together for their services. In this situation, they earned good reputation which gave them huge income benefits. Thus they were able to send significant amounts to their homes. Their life conditions here were better than many other sub-groups, which reflected in their decent living accommodation too.

4.6 Another major ML community was that of painters who composed 09.71 per cent of the total. It had full time and full year job and got smart wages for their specialised work. Since they got good wages, they were able to send good amount to the family members at home. An important feature of this occupational group was that it had heavy component part of children working in the field. Most probably, their service conditions were manipulated and were often exploited by the agents who were responsible for taking them to Kashmir.

4.7 Another category of ML was of the hair-dressers whose proportion was 03.40 per cent of the total. This was one of the most common occupational groups among the BLs. Their presence was prominent in all areas, urban, sub-urban and rural areas. In most of the cases, these hair-dressers replaced the local barbers who left this occupation completely due to occupational mobility. They proved very vocal in their occupation and introduced new-fashionable hair styles and latest techniques. They introduced most of new hair styles among the local youth. So, they became popular and attracted the local youth. Since their occupational activities increased on large scale, they earned huge amount of money and significant portion of that was sent to their homes in Bihar and other states. Majority of them had no or least education and simple minority of them were literate. A very less number of them had formal professional or technical qualification. They had learnt the art of hair cutting either from hereditary sources or from some other informal sources. Many of them had the barbar occupational family background. So, they continued with their family occupation.

4.8 Another category of MLs composed of the occupational groups of cobblers, salesmen on shops and vegetable sellers, who had the proportion of 02.50 per cent, 01.50 per cent and 01.23 per cent of the total respectively. They were comparatively lesser in number but had higher income. They got continuously increasing income in Kashmir and were able to send some amount of money to their homes. While their services were bought for a longer period, they experienced regular and fixed income according to their expectations.

4.9 The last category of MLs composed of tailors, Ice cream sellers, and agricultural laboureRs Their proportion to the total number was 0.95 per cent, 0.53 per cent and 0.42 per cent respectively. The income status of all sub-groups, especially of the tailors sub-group, was good, which enabled them to send enough' money to their homes. They introduced and implemented the old and new techniques in agriculture-horticulture, introduce new fashions in dressing, and earned reasonable income from ice-cream selling. In the category, most of the persons involved were children of 13 - 18 years age group.

5. Professional Qualifications of the ML

5.1. The fact stands with evidence that the whole ML which arrived in Kashmir in all three phases were mostly without any proper and recognised qualification and/or training in the relevant field. Most of them had some kind of idea, experience or informal training in their families which specialised in some occupation. Thus it may be argued that dominant majority of the labour force was either illiterate or had some hereditary occupation training or experience. The employers here in the Kashmir market also didn't demand any formal qualification or experience. They simply trusted on agents who introduced the migrants either as unskilled or skilled and trained or untrained manpower. When we enquired about this aspect among the respondents of this study, their apparent response was shown in the following table:

Table 3.4. Professional-Technical Qualification or Experience of ML

S.No.	*Technical-professional Qualification/experience*	*Number*	*Percentage*
1.	Yes	562	13.38
2.	No	1363	32.92
3.	No response	2255	53.69
	Total	4200	100.00

The table reveals the apparent response of the total number of ML respondents which may not be true. But, we recorded it with certain doubt. A significant group of 32.92 per cent of the total respondents conveyed that they were not qualified or had no formal and recognised training in the area they were working. They arrived in Kashmir without any qualification and training and nobody, even their local employers, enquired about this, though some of them had such qualification, training or experience in their specialised fields, especially tailoring, carpentary, measonary, painting and barbering. In direct contrast to the 1/3 former response, the latter response was conveyed by 13.38 per cent of the total labour force. Even in the case of this trained-experienced manpower, the certificates and/or documents were not demanded either by the local employers or non-local agents. But, not surprisingly, the majority of 53.69 per cent of the total ML didn't show or reveal any response to this question. The most probable explanation of this apparent response can be that it was not correct or true. In actuality, these respondents wanted to hide the reality that they were not qualified or trained or even not literate. Many of them had not got any formal education and many of them were drop outs at the secondary stage. It was also observed that those MLs who were educated, qualified and trained were extremely valued, respected and paid normally higher wage in comparison to their opposite category of the workeRs

6. **Replacement of the Local Labour Force**

6.1. A common but important observation of our researchers was that while the locals considered the local occupations as "degraded", "lower status activities" and "undesirable", the MLs didn't feel on these lines. In that situation, the locals mostly stopped working in these traditional occupations and joined and adopted new occupations such as services, trade and business. On the other side, the alien labour force had no such reservation about these traditional Kashmiri occupations and, so, adopted all of these [occupations] with seriousness, commitment and on continuous basis. In this shunning and adopting processes, while the locals dropped the working in these traditional occupations, the ML force substituted and replaced it systematically and in planned way. Our enquiry in this regard gave us the information that while 25.02 per cent of the total ML had substituted completely the local manpower in many fields/occupations, 50.48 per cent of the total ML had not replaced the local manpower completely but were working side by side with them. It follows that a significant proportion of the local traditional manpower in these occupations was replaced by the ML and on much lower wages than the locals were getting earlier. In reality, the local labour force had consciously and deliberately opted out of these traditional occupations under the grand process of social-occupational mobility and had also opted for new and comparatively maximum profit giving occupations. In this process of occupational mobility, the economic and social criteria were jointly applied in order to give their families a new identity.

7. **Exploitation of the ML**

7.1. It was observed generally that there exists certain degree of exploitation of the ML in their states of origin as well as in Kashmir at the hands of contractors, agents and middlemen. On the one hand, the contractors-agents recruit the labour force in violation of the official norms and procedures and no written documents are made with them. The former recruit the labour force verbally and on very less rates and engage even the child labourers for some particular period by providing some meager amount of advance to their parents. In this way, this labour force arrived

Kashmir without any formal commitment to service, job, amount of salary, period of stay here, and so on. On the other hand, the local employers remain silent on the wages and child labour issues. They too do not pay just and deserving wages to the labourers in general and child labourers in particular. Thus the local employers also exploit the general labour force and child labour in particular. The latter are not paid in person in most of the cases but their wages are sent to their parents. In addition, the workers are compelled to work for more than normal hours and to work on weekly holidays also. Our researchers' observation found that there prevails a clear situation of exploitation on the part of agents and employers, especially of the child laboureRs When we enquired about this matter from the respondents, their response was as has been noted in the table below:

Table 3. 5. Does Exploitation of ML exists

S. No.	*Does exploitation exists*	*Number*	*Percentage*
1.	Yes	162	03.85
2.	No	2029	48.30
3.	No response	2009	47.84
	Total	4200	100.00

The above table reveals completely different response from the response received through research investigators' observation. While majority of the respondents deny any degree of exploitation or imposition of forceful practices on them, the researchers found significant degree of exploitation of the ML, especially of its child component, in Kashmir. It may be explained that since majority of the MLs arrived here without any formal documents and children were also involved in this work, they got exploited necessarily and in any case.

7.2. The above table reveals that while 03.85 per cent respondents agreed with the proposition that some degree of exploitation exists among Migrant labourers, 48.30 per cent respondents gave the opposite views, i.e., they were not exploited at all. This response seems fully fictitious in order to hide the actual reality of exploitation. The other such response of 47.84 per cent falls in the same category of response. This response represents the effort to hide the related to the exploitation of labour force. In their view, they played safe by hiding the facts. They also wanted to save the contractors, agents and employers involved in this practice. They fear that there is every possibility of throwing them out of job if the role of these exploiters was exposed to the police or any other agency.

8. Motivation by Different Individuals

8.1. It seems very clear that the MLs were contacted and motivated by different individuals in their home states who included their family members, near relatives, neighbours and family friends. Subsequently, they migrated to Kashmir by themselves or with the help provided by contractors, agents and otheRs There were very less number of agencies which are engaged in this type of migration as per official laws, legal practices and legal procedure. In actuality, there existed an informal and completely unofficial arrangement of recruiting the labourers on verbal promises. No written details and documents were involved in this type of arrangement of the laboureRs Apparently, it suited both, the contractors-agents and illiterate laboureRs In an enquiry about this matter, we got the response noted in the following table:

Table 3. 6. Individuals who motivated labourers to migrate

S. No.	*Individual who motivated*	*Number*	*Percentage*
1.	Contractors	723	17.21
2.	Agents	650	15.70
3.	Employers	660	16.00
4.	Other individuals [family members-Friends, neighbours and relatives]	2149	51.16
5.	No response	18	00.42
	Total	4200	100.00

The above table reveals that there was the plurality of individuals who motivated and then sent thousands of labourers to Kashmir to work and earn more amount of money than used to earn at their own places. The individuals such as family members, family friends, near and distant relatives and neighbours, composed of the first dominant group which motivated on different basis to migrate to Kashmir and work there for some time. They composed 51.16 per cent of the total respondents. This contact was based on personal or family relations. When an individual arrived in Kashmir for work and felt convinced about the normalcy of the situation, he called others who primarily included family members, friends, neighbours and acquaintances. In this way, a lot of MLs came to Kashmir and worked here. They usually worked in groups and stayed together. They used to come to Kashmir and go for break together. They shared and enjoyed their cultural life in an alien place.

8.2. The second group of individuals who motivated MLs to go to Kashmir to work for earning more income were contractors, agents and employeRs They did this operation individually or in cooperation with each other. Their contribution was identified in the cases of 17.21 per cent, 15.70 per cent and 16.00 per cent of the total number of MLs. They recruited the labourers in home states under certain unwritten procedure and took them to Kashmir. All three groups were business like people who charged their commission and left them in Kashmir. Here the employers also provided cooperation in this process. They were not concerned about the life conditions, job conditions, exploitation of the labourers, especially the child labourers, safety and security of MLs and other related matteRs

9. Immediate Consequences of Migration at Home

9.1. After working for several years, the MLs were able to save some amount of money which they sent necessarily to their homes in places of origin. This increased income didn't help in the improvement of life conditions of MLs only, but their families also. It was reported that there was significant and obvious improvement in life conditions at'the homes of migrants, as the increased income reached them and they spent on education, standard diet, health, and other crucial life needs. It was also observed that the migrants' money transformed the entire life of their families in their places of origin. On our inquiry regarding the immediate needs and priority areas on which the migrants money was spent [that led to improvement in standard of life], we got the responses noted in the table below:

Table 3. 7. Priority Areas on which Migrants' money was spent by concerned families

S. No.	*Priority Area of Investment*	*Number*	*Percentage*
1.	Improvement in life style/standard	1178	28.04
2.	Family needs on the whole	647	15.40
3.	Construction works/homes	621	14.99
4.	Education of children	504	12.86
5.	Miscellaneous purposes	383	09.12
6.	Marriage of child/children	245	05.84
7.	Savings in the local banks	230	05.48
8.	Buying land for house/family	227	05.40
9.	Health problems and health care	129	03.07
	Total	4200	100.00

The above table clearly indicates that there was overall improvement in the life conditions of ML families at their places of origin in different states. Since the significant amount of money was sent to the homes of MLs, this pattern of investment had striking impact on the entire life of home people. The family members there spent the money according to their short and long term needs and priority areas. So, there emerged different patterns of the investment of this money. The first priority area of this investment was to enhance the standard of life in their families, as was revealed by a dominant majority of 1178 out of 4200 [i.e., 28.04 per cent of the total] respondents. This investment was highly needed in the context of extreme poverty which existed in these families earlier or in the past. Thus it may be argued that there was experienced considerable improvement in the standard of life mainly due to increased income of the ML in Kashmir and its transfer to their homes in their home states, particularly Bihar.

9.2. The second area of investment and its potential consequences was related to the family's short and long term needs which stood different for different families. 647/4200 [i.e., 15.40 per cent of the total] respondents made this type of investment which included large investment for home items and small expenditure for daily-need items. The nature of this expenditure/investment was such that it reflected in the overall mobility and family lifestyle.

9.3. The third area of expenditure of the ML's money was the construction sector in which houses, shops and other business establishments were established. According to 621/4200 [i.e., 14.98 per cent] respondents, they invested the hard-earned money in much needed sector of construction of residential houses. It follows that most of the MLs had no house of their own or lived in rented accommodation or in slums. Now, after working in Kashmir for some years, they were in a position to accumulate an amount which enabled them to purchase of minimum size of land and construct a residential house over it or purchase of the house. In this regard, 227/4200 [i.e., 05.40 per cent of the total] respondents conveyed that their primary priority was to purchase land for constructing their own house. Some of them were successful in converting this dream into a reality. In this context, they considered that the purchase of land and construction of residential house was possibly because of their work in Kashmir for many years Thus this pattern of migrants' investment in their home states proved the factor of stability and improvement in their lifestyle and general quality of life.

9.4. Education of children was other area of investment of the MLs money at their homes. 504/4200 [i.e., 12.86 per cent of the total] respondents conveyed that a significant portion of their shifted money was spent by their families on the education of their children both boys and girls and in reputed schools. It seems important to note that all these children were not able to get even primary education in the past mainly due to extreme poverty situation. But, that situation has changed for them now. Since the MLs earned and saved some money, that enabled their families to send their children to schools. Thus it has been established that the higher wages of labour force in Kashmir enabled ML save money, which enabled them to send their children for modern education in their home states. These children seem to represent the first literate generation in their families.

9.5. 383/4200 [i.e., 09.12 per cent of the total] respondents revealed that the money they sent to homes enabled them to make expenditure in unconventional fields. These new areas of expenditure included purchase of consumer-luxurious items, consumption of lavish foods, buying dresses and various hobby-entertainment and IT items. They have also become the consumers of globalised IT and high-technology items available in the market.

9.6. The next item of expenditure at home was related to children's marriage expenses, i.e., expenditure before, during and after marriage rituals and practices. In order to formalise and celebrate the marriage of their children, especially of daughters, they spend heavy amounts earned in Kashmir. Though this was not in vogue in the past due to poverty, the recent economic mobility enabled them now to spend for these rituals and celebrations. 245/4200 [05.80 per cent of the total] respondents conveyed that they spent considerable amount of money for marriage-related expenditure of their children. Thus they spent lavishly on marriages, which was not possible in the past.

9.7. Another area of expenditure at home was savings in the banks. This was exclusively new and unprecedented area of expenditure. Earlier they were illiterate and were neither aware nor committed to the savings in banks. But, in the present conditions in which they have earned extra money and thus were able to make savings in different banks in their respective states. 230/4200 [i.e., 05.48 per cent of the total] respondents provided this information that they had deposits in different nationalised banks. This reflects a serious transformation of sociological importance and became a source of change in other fields of life.

9.8. Another significant area of expenditure was identified as 'health problems and healthcare. This expenditure was crucial and long and short term implications of MLs and their families. It represented an unconventional and unprecedented attitude towards normal health on the part of the concerned families. It certainly led processes of health improvement of all members of the families. It represented an important development partly because they were not able to approach the proper medical care in the past due to extreme poverty and partly because they were able to take care of their health in the present situation mainly due to their enhanced income. In this situational background, 129/4200 [i.e., 03.07 per cent of the total] respondents conveyed that their families made an expenditure on consultation of expert doctors, various diagonastic tests, purchase of medicines, and general health care. They also upheld that this was not possible for their own generation about 50 years back. About 4 per cent of the total regular expenditure on health care stands as the desirable variable for a standard health.

9.9. Thus it reveals clearly from the above explanation and with statistical support that the extra money earned by MLs had transformed the existing life conditions of their families significantly in their respective states of origin. In this context, one may presume that the economic mobility of the MLs had certainly transformed the quality, standard and conditions of their families. This economic mobility and its immediate impact stands comparable with such other cases in the country.

11. Increasing Income and Increasing Mobility of ML

11.1. The relationship between the increasing income of MLs and their total mobility, especially of economic nature, in life revealed in the respondents' response which is shown in the following table:

Table 3. 8. Increasing Income and Increasing Mobility of ML

S. No.	*Response*	*Increase in Income*		*Increase in Mobility*	
		Number	*Percentage*	*Number*	*Percentage*
1.	Yes	3029	72.00	2568	61.00
2.	No	1008	24.00	1100	26.19
3.	No response	168	4.00	532	13.00
	Total	4200	100.00	4200	100.00

The preceding table shows clearly the intimate and reciprocal relationship between increased income of the ML and increase in mobility in totality among huge majority of respondents' families. Theoretically, it may be argued that economy plays the basic and dominant role. So, with improvement in the economic field and consequent affluence, an overall mobility pattern was necessarily associated with it. This may be observed in the life style and life standard prevailing in the ML families now. Thus it seems very easy to explain the reciprocal relationship between the responses of 3024/4200 [i.e., 72.00 of the total] and 2568/4200 [i.e., 61.00 per cent of the total] respondents. While the former response represented the increase in income, the latter response gave information about overall mobility in life. In this way, some among this category of ML were able to enter in to the status of middle class or lower middle class.

11.2. On the other hand, the above table also reveals that there seems a negative co-relation between economic mobility and overall mobility. In our investigation, while 1008/4200 [24.00 per cent of the total] respondents did not increase their income, 1100/4200 [i.e., 26.19 per cent of the total] respondents also didn't experience overall mobility in economic and social fields. In actuality, both these responses have to be seen in the relevant context. They don't means that there is no necessary and intimate relationship between economic and overall mobility. In fact, they want to highlight the role of other factors in this process. Moreover, these respondents had not undergone fully the process of radical transformation in life.

12. Amount of Expenditure by the ML in Kashmir

12.1. As stands clear from the situation, the ML had to spend some amount of their income on their daily-life needs such as food, clothes, transport and rent. This study revealed that ML had to spend some amount, though very less proportion of their income, for their daily life items and needs. It was generally felt that they didn't maintain a high standard of life while staying in Kashmir. But, the minimum standard which they maintained here during their period of stay was better than what they had in their home states before migration to Kashmir on the one hand and was much inferior than the locals' standard on the other hand. Thus they had to spend a smaller amount of income on some items or fields. The details in this regard are noted in the following table:

Table 3. 9. Details about Daily-use Items and Amount of Expenditure

S.No.	*Daily use Items*	*Percentage of amount spent in local market*
1.	Rent for joint-group accommodation	20.00 per cent
2.	Food and drink items	19.52 per cent
3.	Transport expenses	20.45 per cent
4.	Dresses and clothes	19.03 per cent
5.	Bidis and Chunna toxicants	10.00 per cent
6.	Other items of daily life use	11.00 per cent
	Total	100.00 per cent

It follows from the table that the MLs spent some amount of their income [which was always more than their actual needs] in six major fields in more or less equal proportion. These were the fields in which they had to pay necessarily without which they could not have survived in Kashmir. While this amount came from the pockets of MLs and went in the pockets of locals. This stands probably the only material benefit which the local community availed from the presence of huge ML force.

12.2. In our study, we made a qualitative investigation regarding the amount which the MLs spent in Kashmir during their stay and work here. In response to this enquiry, we got detailed information recorded in the table which follows:

Table 3. 10. Nature of Expenditure by the ML in Kashmir

S.No.	*Field*	*Expenditure [Rs p.m.]*	*Number*	*Percentage*
1.	Rent of accommodation	below 500	430	10.24
		501 - 1000	300	07.14
		1001 - 1500	110	02.62
		Not paid	00	00.00
2.	Food items	below 500	410	09.76
		501 - 1000	300	07.14
		1001 - 1500	110	02.62
		Not paid	00	00.00
3.	Transport charges	below 500	400	09.52
		501 - 1000	300	07.14
		1001 - 1500	90	02.14
		not paid	70	01.67
4.	Dresses	below 500	500	11.90
		501 - 1000	300	07.14
		1001 - 1500	00	00.00
		not paid	00	00.00
5.	Other daily expenses	below 500	50	01.19
		501 - 1000	20	00.48
		1001 - 1500	00	00.00
		not paid	00	00.00
6.	Misc. expenditure	below 500	450	10.71
		501 - 1000	360	08.57
		1001 - 1500	00	00.00
		not paid	00	00.00
		Total	4200	100.00

The above table reveals six major heads of expenditure during their stay-work in Kashmir, the detailed explanation of which follows:

[a] *Rent for Joint/Shared Accommodation:* While 430/4200 [i.e.,10.24 per cent of the total] respondents spent an amount of less than Rs 500 per month for rented accommodation in urban and rural areas, 300/4200 [07.14 per cent of the total] respondents had to pay an amount between 500 to 1000 per month for the same purpose. Since near total majority of ML lived in joint/shared accommodation, usually composed of one/two big room/s or dormitory, they had to pay such a lesser amount. Only 02.62 per cent of the total respondents had to pay 1000 to 1500 per month for their rent and this higher amount was prevalent in urban than in rural areas. None among the respondents revealed that he got rent free accommodation, though some of them got it from their employeRs Some were also given rooms with the employer's house.

[b] In the case of food items, while 410/4200 [i.e., 09.76 per cent of the total] respondents spent below 500 per month, 300/4200 [i.e., 07.14 per cent of the total] respondents paid 500 to 1000 per month for the same purpose. This amount stands lesser and cheaper. The MLs usually prepared rice, dal and vegetables which all were low cost varieties. Finally, 110/4200 [i.e., 2.62 per cent of the total] respondents paid an amount between 1000 - 1500 per month for food items.

[c] In the case of transport charges, while 400/4200 [i.e., 09.52 per cent of the total] respondents had to pay below 500 per month, 300/4200 [i.e., 07.14 per cent of the total] respondents spent 500 1000 per month for the same purpose. Both these charges were relative lower charges in the local transport which stands costly in comparison to other cities in the country. 02.14 per cent of the total respondents had to pay an amount between 1000 to 1500 mainly because they had to travel far off places or peripheries of the city for their work. Finally, 70/4200 [i.e., 01.67 per cent of the total] respondents had not to pay any amount for transport as this was provided by the employer or contractor and they took them to work sites and back to their residences.

[d] For their dresses, the ML had to spend less than 500 per month in the case of 500/4200 [i.e., 11.90 per cent of the total respondents and 500 to 1000 in the case of 300 [i.e., 7.14 per cent of the total]

respondents. They always used old and shabby dresses and hardly washed these clothes. They also didn't purchase new clothes, except on the religious occasions and festivals. So, the bill on account of dress was lowest.

[e] 50/4200 [i.e., 01.19 per cent of the total] respondents made expenditure on account of purchase of daily-use items like soaps, detergents and tooth paste. These items also included heavy number of biddies, cigrattes, gutka, choona and other toxic substances which they consume regularly without any break. Many of them consume local 'thera' or wine and use drugs repeatedly. 20/4200 [i.e., 00.48 per cent of the total] respondents spent 500 to 1000 per month for these purposes.

[f] In terms of the misc. expenditure, while 450/4200 [i.e., 10.71 per cent of the total] respondents spent less than 500 per month, 360/4200 [i.e., 08.57 per cent of the total] respondents had to pay 500 to 1000 per month.

13. Interaction with the Host Society

13.1. After their arrival and settlement in Kashmir, the ML had to interact necessarily with members and culture of the host society. This interaction between locals and aliens may lead to positive as well as to negative type of relationship between the two communities. It focuses on attitudes and behaviour of the ML on the one hand and approach and treatment on the part of local employers and local people. In totality, the response of the host society was determined by the mass behaviour of MLs and other socio-economic factoRs In the specific environment of Kashmir, a particular type of relationship between migrants and the locals emerged which can be characterised by peace as well as conflict between the two. While the positive relationship developed by economic, cultural, religious and social factors, the negative relationship was the result of economic, social and cultural abnormalities of the migrants. This type of relationship determined the stay of ML in Kashmir. When enquired from the respondents in this regard, they provided the following response:

[i] positive relationship 2634/4200 [62.71 per cent of the total] respondents

[ii] negative relationship 1280/4200 [30.49 per cent of the total] respondents

13.2. The first type of interaction and resultant type of relationship was based on positive ideas, opinions, impressions, perceptions and experiences and generally led to cordial and harmonious relations between two separate communities. On the other hand, the second type of interaction and consequent relationship was based on negative ideas, opinions, perceptions, views and experiences, which gave birth to non-cordial and disharmonious type of relations.

13.3. Again, in the same social and cultural background, the ML community got positive or negative image/impression of the locals and local culture. In this context, they either appreciated or didn't appreciate the locals and their culture. These early images and the impressions of the locals get set in the minds of the migrants and they mention these not in front of the locals but in their own private meetings. Our investigation in this connection revealed that 2634/4200 [i.e., 62.71 per cent of the total] respondents had positive experiences, while 1280/4200 [i.e., 30.49 per cent of the total] respondents had the negative experiences. The first kind of response gave rise to cordial relations with the local families where MLs were treated well and respected. On the other hand, the second response led to disharmony and hostility between the migrant and host communities. They had developed no family ties with the local families, lived in isolation and developed a kind of negative attitude against the locals.

13.4. Here it seems important that a significant proportion of the respondents, i.e., 39.04 per cent of the total number of respondents didn't respond to this question/theme and avoided to put forth their particular views and opinions. It can be inferred from the actual situation that majority of these respondents had no liking for the local culture for a variety of reasons, which vary from personal to social and from economic to cultural reasons. However, they developed a common type of disassociation and antagonism against the local culture. However, a little minority among MLs liked and appreciated the local cultural traits and personality. They had no grudge or misgiving about the local cultural kinds.

13.5. At the same time, it is also important to mention here that the majority of ML developed a dual attitude towards the local culture and local people. It was the attitude according to which they appreciated and praised the local culture in the open but condemned and criticised it in their private meetings. This behaviour was adopted in view of the reaction on the part of local employers and people. So, they played safe choice in order to avoid the adverse local reaction and retaliation. This silence can be characterised as strategic. For a detailed debate about migrant-local relationship, see *Greater Kashmir*, Srinagar, July 7, 2003 and August 5, 2003.

14. Migration Impact on Physical and Mental Health

14.1. As it is clear from every aspect of this situation, the migration of labourers from different states of India had influenced some or whole of their lives from physical to mental health. So, we made investigation in this regard. The response was as mentioned below:

[i] Positive impact on health

1074/4200 [25.58 1074/4200 [25.58 per cent]] of the total respondents;

[ii] Negative impact on health

1406/4200 [33.47 per cent] of the total respondents;

[iii] No response

1720/4200 [40.95 per cent] of the total respondents.

These three responses represent three different reactions of the ML. First, about a quarter of respondents, i.e., 1074/4200 [25.58 per cent] of the total], had felt a positive impact on their health in Kashmir. In this response, they conveyed certain points which are:

[a] they had stable health condition before migrating to Kashmir and they maintained this stable condition even after migration despite different weather conditions;

[b] their health had not deteriorated to such a level where the consultation or advice of doctor was unavoidable;

[c] they had to spend less or very less amount of money on health care and health problems;

[d] they developed no particular disease/s in Kashmir and some of them reported summer-heat related diseases did not occur in Kashmir;

[e] they developed certain degree of resistance after migration in Kashmir and they could bear even harsh winter conditions here. This view was presented particularly by those migrants who stayed here for the whole year.

14.2. However, even in these conditions, 1406/4200 [i.e., 33.47 per cent of the total] respondents reported negative impact of migration on their health. They conveyed some specific points which include the following:

[a] the migrants fell ill several times due to one or other reason;

[b] they had consulted the private or hospital doctors to whom they paid good amount of money for their treatment;

[c] they could not develop a sufficient degree of resistance to all/ various diseases in the harsh winter conditions of Kashmir. So, they often feel ill and diseased;

[d] the local weather conditions had adverse and deteriorating effect on the lives of the migrants.

14.3. The third opinion of "no response" was conveyed by 1720/4200 [i.e., 40.95 per cent of the total] respondents. On the basis of experience and understanding of the relevant situation, it may be inferred that majority of them was not feeling stable, fit and normal physically as well as mentally and in the complete sense. This occurs during their continuous stay in harsh weather conditions in Kashmir. On the other hand, many among them were physical and mentally fit and remained so in Kashmir too. But, the fact stands that seasonal ups and down disturbs more or less all of them. The general trend among them was that they didn't want to divulge information about the actual mental and physical health. They fear some negative repercussion because of this disclosure on their part.

14.4 At the same time, we enquired specifically about mental health condition of ML. It was mainly because, after migrating to Kashmir, they found themselves in an alien world which they had never encountered and had to adjust in entirely different ethos, environment and conditions. It was observed that the process of adjustment or adoption and socialisation in new social order put them to difficulties and problems. This process of adoption or adjustment had direct relationship with the mental makeup up of the MLs. So, while some of them adjusted fast, others adjusted slowly and still many others didn't adjust and remained mentally disturbed. Moreover, the mental health of their ML was determined by the tenure, quality, income, output of their work in Kashmir. When we enquired about these aspects of the mental health, their response is noted below:

[i] mentally stable and satisfactory
532/4200 [12.66 per cent of the total]

[ii] Mentally not stable and not satisfactory
1963/4200 [46.73 per cent of the total]

[iii] no response
1705/4200 [40.60 per cent of the total]

14.5. The first response conveyed by 532/4200 [i.e., 12.66 per cent of the total] respondents showed the stable and satisfactory mental condition. This small number generally belonged to the mature age and married groups. In comparison to a large number of youth, these elder and experienced respondents had worked in Kashmir for more time and had enough interaction and positive relationship with the local community. They also appreciated many features of the local culture and social order.

14.6. The second response nearly half of the total of 1963/4200 [i.e., 46.74 per cent of the total] respondents revealed that they were neither stable nor satisfactory mentally. They usually belonged to younger age groups and had arrived Kashmir in recent years only. Their less experience and lesser interaction with the local community didn't allow them to develop stable and satisfied mental conditions. It took them some time to settle down in new working, social and cultural conditions in Kashmir.

14.7. The 1705/4200 [i.e., 40. 60 per cent of the total] respondents did not express their opinion in regard to mental and physical health. However, on the basis of experience, one may state that while half of them were mentally stable and the other half of them were in the opposite condition. It led to long-term stay in Kashmir in the case of former and short-term stay in the case of latter. It was observed that some of the cases among the latter category deteriorated and some among them had to return to their homes. All of them had to consult the expert doctors in state or private sector, but some of them resorted to the use of drugs which invited locals' criticism against them.

15. The Trade Union Contact

15.1. It was generally felt that there was no trade union activity and no formal contact with the trade union movement. It was mainly because they were working purely on temporary basis and on the local employers' sweet will. Moreover, they were not in a position to displease the local employers and authorities and were not also to bargain with them at all. They had accepted what was offered to them on their arrival. The MLs at large had a strong feeling that they were working in a non-local/alien place and, so, nobody can come to their support or help in case some problem or dispute arises related to trade union activity. In this context, they remained completely aloof from trade union activities in Kashmir. In our investigation, more or less same types of responses were conveyed by respondents, which are showed in the following:

[i] involvement in trade union activities

01.60 per cent of the total respondents

[ii] no involvement in trade union activities

41.02 per cent of the total respondents

[iii] no response

57.38 per cent of the total respondents

The second and third responses can be clubbed together, i.e., 41.02 per cent + 57.38 per cent = 99.40. That leads to the proposition that near total of respondents were not participating or involved in any kind of trade union activity at their places of work. They had no intention of their involvement in these activities in future too. On the other hand, only extreme-micro level group of 1.60 per cent of the total respondents were active in this type of activities. In reality, these activities were of social, cultural, economic and trade union type of activities.

16. Major Problems at Places of Work faced by the MLs

16.1. It was observed that the MLs at large faced certain serious problems at their places of work in Kashmir after they came and worked there for some time. All labourers faced these or some of these problems irrespective of their field of work and status of work. They were highly conscious about these problems and wanted to resolve fully as early as possible. Our investigation in this regard gave us the information recorded in the table below:

Table 3.11. Major Problems at Places of Work faced by the MLs

S. No.	*Nature of Problem*	*Number*	*Percentage*
1.	Accommodation Problems	1279	30.45
2.	Health problems	610	14.53
3.	Child labour problems	550	13.27
4.	Beggary problems	501	11.93
5.	Drug addiction	400	09.06
6.	Wine consumption problems	380	09.05
7.	Other problems	480	11.42
	Total	4200	100.00

The preceding table reveals that the ML in Kashmir faced many problems among which some were most crucial for their work and stay here. So, this enormity of concerned problems contributed to their long or short stay in Kashmir. Our investigation in this connection revealed that seven sets of problems were identified by them and were considered as serious and major problems. First, the most difficult problem all MLs faced in Kashmir just after their arrival was directly related to their accommodation. In fact, every member of ML community faced this problem. This was partly because of scaresity of rented places in the city and towns and partly because relatively higher amount of rent was demanded in these areas. Most of migrants wanted cheaper and joint accommodation. In order to pay the least amount of rent, they usually got together and shared the dormitory-type or other joint-type accommodation in which more than 3 or 4 persons could be accommodated. In this way, they got minimum accommodation of shared nature on minimum rates.

16.2. The second major and serious problem which the MLs faced was related to their mental and physical health. This problem which they could not avoid was caused mainly because of extremely different weather conditions in Kashmir and different social, cultural, religious and economic conditions. In this new environment, they could not maintain balance mentally and physically. On the one hand, they could not develop mental health balance due to social-cultural differences and on the other hand could not maintain physical balance due to weather/seasonal environment. This situation was conveyed by 610/4200 [i.e., 14. 53 per cent of the total] respondents. Most of them had to consult the private health clinics or state hospitals where doctors treated them.

16.3. The third problem faced by 550/4200 [i.e., 13.20 per cent of the total] respondents was related to child labour. In fact, it reflected the serious and severe concern of elder age groups about the child/younger age child labourers in terms of lowest wages, more work at work place, no holidays and so on. It generally led to their exploitation at the hands of employers and agents and contractoRs These child labourers were taken from their homes in places of origin in undesirable conditions and non-voluntarily by paying some meager amount to their parents for an undecided period. Here at their work places, they were treated well in ideal conditions and lived and worked in conditions characteristic of the phenomenon of exploitation.

16.4. The fourth problem of beggary was conveyed by 501/4200 [i.e., 11.13 per cent of the total] respondents. It follows that when MLs arrived here with their families and settled in slums in different cities and towns. The men of these families used to go for daily work at the work sites and other members, particularly women and small children, used to go for begging. When a large number of these people joined the begging activity, it emerged as a social problem for the locals who had criticised them for this curse.

16.5. The fifth problem identified by 400/4200 [09.06 per cent of the total] respondents was drug addiction. Consequently, the unskilled labour and their families used cheap drugs available at their home market and at the locals markets too. Not only drugs were used regularly by these MLs, they also sold variety of drugs to the local youth who became drug addicts after some time. [See also Greater Kashmir, Srinagar, 29 June, 2012]

16.6. The 11.42 per cent of the total respondents faced other problems which were related to personal, social, economic, cultural problems and worst work conditions prevailing in Kashmir.

6

Different Migration Trends and their Social Impact on Women in J&K

1. Like other societies in the country, the society in J&K has experienced widespread change, especially among the specific groups and communities of women primarily due to long-term implications of migration. Though the nature and degree of this impact varied, it affected all concerned/ involved groups of women in the state. Before explaining the specific impact of migration on women in J&K, it seems necessary that the patterns of impact of migration which prevails in the areas of Indo-Nepal and Indo-Bangladesh international borders does not exist on the borders of J&K, even on 'Line of control' called LOC. Both the borders with Pakistan are patrolled by the armies of both countries so heavily and intensively that cross border traffickking seems just impossible. In addition to fighting three wars on these borders, the conflict between India and Pakistan always keep these borders hot, volatile and difficult for even minimum human activity or movement.
2. However, the impact of migration, especially on women, in the state has occurred and observed in different sociological context. Several studies on the nature and impact of migration in the state have been carried out by the concerned experts.
3. This author has carried out two empirical-sociological studies in the state in the past and present decades. The first study was carried out in late 1990s in ten districts of Kashmir province which are as follows:

[i]	Srinagar	[ii]	Anantnag
[iii]	Baramulla	[iv]	Budgam
[v]	Pulwama	[vi]	Kupwara
[vii]	Ganderbal	[viii]	Bandipora
[ix]	Kulgam	[x]	Shopian

The second study was carried out in four districts of Jammu province which are as follows:

[i]	Udhampur	[ii]	Samba
[iii]	Jammu	[iv]	Kathua

4. While the first study concentrated on women of KPs living in Jammu migrant camps or residential houses or government accommodation, the second study was concentrated mainly on the migrants who are in lakhs present in the Kashmir valley and belong to the states of Bihar, U.P., Rajasthan, West Bengal and Madhya Pradesh. These skilled, semi-skilled and unskilled workers in all occupational fields started coming here in the decade of 1980s and have increased their number heavily over the years As a result of these developments, while they have taken over completely from the locals some occupations such as barber, meason and painting, they have dominated other occupations in the valley. These migrant labourers work and earn a significant amount of money in J&K must have certainly led to some degree of change and mobility among their family members at their homes. But, presence of them along with their family in Kashmir has contributed positively as well as negatively.

5. The broader and prominent findings of the study of impact of migration on the KP women include the below-mentioned:

   [i] The KPs have traditionally remained an 'endogamous group'. It follows that they usually married their sons and daughters within their own caste or kin group. But, after masss migration from Kashmir in 1990-91, this pattern and its related practices faced a serious challenge. It was partly because most of the KP boys left for outside state for educational and employment purposes and partly because commitment to endogamy could not be maintained strictly in urbanising-industrialising and migration environment. It that situation, the Pandit girls had to adopt the practice of exogamy and marry outside the traditional endogamous caste-kin group. Thus many among them were married to non-Kashmiri boys living in different cities and towns in India. Some among them were married even to the boys of the south Indian region who maintain extreme differences.

   [ii] In the post-migration situation, the practices of 'hypergamy' [marriage between the boy of higher caste status and the girl of lower caste status]lost their relevance and primacy. Now, the

primacy and for selecting/marrying a boy or a girl had shifted to the criteria of education, employment, living/available accommodation and so on. Thus KP women entered into a non-conventional situation vis-à-vis the marriage market. This shift in preferences had definite implications for KP women in their post-marital life.

[iii] Patrilocality [a practice in which the boy takes the girl to his house and settle there for whole life after marriage] was other commom practice among the KPs. But, due to mass migration from Kashmir, and accommodation problems at new places of settlement like Jammu, some of them opted for the practice of 'matrilocality'. It follows that KP boys settled at girls' houses after their marriage. Though this new practice was introduced/initiated but not in a big way and for long time or for ever. Usually, this practice was adopted for a short period till the married couple got their own accommodation. However, in a matri-local type of social set-up, women generally developed some plus points vis-à-vis their husbands and their families.

[iv] Migration helped the KP migrant women in the educational advancement qualitatively as well as quantitatively. While migration proved the motivating factor for pursueing higher education. At the same time, the offers of reservation by some state governments helped the KP women to go for higher professional and technical education with financial assistance. It may not be out of context to mention that KP community stands already 100 percent literate. They maintained this educational status even after migration and despite living in the camps. In fact, they made improvements in this regard .

[v] The KPs in general had availed all employment opportunities in J&K mainly due to their educational advancement. They maintained this highest record even after mass migration in the case of males as well as females. Despite this positive situation, KPs faced the problem of unemployment significantly and women shared this problem more than men. The female unemployment rate has increased considerably in the previous decades.

[vi] In the post-migration period, though the KP women faced several severe problems, they maintained a certain degree of educational-economic-social mobility even in difficult conditions. In other words, despite tough life in the migrant camps in the Jammu city,

they worked very hard to maintain certain level of mobility in more and more fields of life.

[vii] After they migrated from the Kashmir valley in 1990-91, where they upheld completely traditional cultural life pattern, the cultural exposure was a common and necessary phenomenon for all KP women. Now, outside Kashmir after undergoing migration, they lived like and interact with non-Kashmiri cultural groups and communities in different cities and towns in the country. In this processs of interaction, the adoption of non-Kashmiri cultural traits/ features, especially in the field of language, dress, lifestyle, religious practices and so on became inevitable for them.

[viii] The KP women suffered in the early period of post-migration era in the field of 'reproductive health practices'. It was found by experts that they could not maintain normal reproductive practice such as procreation and delivery of child. In the situation of over-crowding in the migrant camps and one room flats, the normal sex behaviour was seriously disturbed which affected their normal health. This also certainly affected the growth rate/s and age-sex composition of population at the community level.

[ix] The KP women developed many health problems primarily due to migration and its impact. The extreme hot weather conditions outside Kashmir was one basic factor for this situation. In addition to sun strokes and snake bites, they faced other dreaded diseases like neurological-heart diseases, hyper-tension and many psychological problems.

6. On the other hand, the major findings of the study about the 'impact of migration on women among Bihari Migrant Labour' [BML] were as mentioned below:

[i] The basic fact related to the BML was that it led to the fulfillment of all or basic needs of their women and children at their homes. This economic benefit has materialised in the context of skilled and unskilled labour who migrated to Kashmir single-handedly and send their earned money to their homes regularly. Most of these labourers come here in March and leave in November. Thus they earn money and serve their families during the winter months.

[ii] Near total majority of migrants in J&K live a life of 'cultural aloofness'. It means that, culturally and socially, they hardly interact with the local population. In actuality, they live in 'separate social clusters' and practice their home culture/s, especially in terms of language, dress, attitudes. Life-style, behviour patterns, entertainment, consumer expenditure, food habits and religious practices. In this process, the families of migrants, especially their women, have provided necessary inspiration and support. So, they have proved instrumental in this cultural and social changes.

[iii] The economic role of the migrant women at large has proved not productive for themselves in Kashmir. It was because their income [which they earn from their self work in Kashmir] was not retained with them, nor was it spent on their needs only. Actually, their entire income was grabbed by their husbands [or by any other male member in the family] and usually spent according to their own choices, preferences and priorities. In this list, the welfare of womenfolk figured in the last or not at all. In this way, though the migrant women worked side by side with their men and earned a fair amount, it didn't prove useful and beneficial to them.

[iv] Besides economic exploitation, the majority of migrant women were exploited in the social sphere too. Since they and their families live in 'migrant clusters' away from home and from patri-kins, they were totally dependent on their husbands and their male relatives. In that situation, they were usually mal-treated, abused, mentally as well as physically, by their husbands. In some cases, they were often beaten physically and compelled to carry out even undesirable and illegal activities.

[v] Dominant majority of BML has established the slums in the city and towns and lived a 'pathetic and miserable' life there. It is believed that there were no slums in the city of Srinagar some decades back. But, many slums have emerged on the peripheries of cities and towns. The sub-human living conditions in these slums have been the reasons to many health and environment problems. The social-cultural ethos of the slums has been polluted to a considerable level.

[vi] It was observed that migrant women in Kashmir have been involved directly or indirectly to prepare or produce the local varieties of wine and drugs and were spread among the local youth.

[v] The BML in J&K was composed of a significant number of child labourers working in many sectoRs They, especially the female child labourers, were paid very less wages and were exploited. It was observed that many such migrant labourers were harassed, molested and even raped, not only by others but by relatives also. As per reports, the BML seniors have been involved in various practices of child labour racket. According to reports, many children were taken to Kashmir after their parents were paid petty sums in lieu of their children for years together. This stood clearly in violation of rules and laws of the state as well as the centre. The agents and '*thekedars*' of Bihar are directly involved in these scandles of child labour.

[vi] The BML presence in Kashmir has given rise to organised and unorganised begging on the part of their children. While the organised begging was based in the slums from where groups of child beggers were recuited, trained, organised, sponsored and monitored by the criminal elements and gangs, the unorganised beggers, especially female were also based in the slums but are directly connected the 'begging network'. In addition, because of tourist destination, Kashmir attracts a large number of BML in the guise of tourists during the tourist season.

[vii] In the situation mentioned above, delinquency, crime and prostitution were the natural consequence. It was observed that migrant labourers, especially women, were directly or indirectly contributing to this pathological situation. Thus the crime graph in Kashmir has gone up to the alarming level, in which the contribution of migrant women was significant. At many times, according to the local news reports, several sex rackets were exposed in which the migrant women were always involved.

[viii] In the worst living conditions of the BML in the slums in Srinagar and in other towns, emergence of acute and dangerous problems of health could neither be avoided nor controlled effectively. Special

mention may be made about heavy increase in the cases of HIV and other communicable diseases.

[ix] Due to these activities on the part of BML, especially migrant women, a situation of social tension has arisen between migrant labour community and the local population. This situation has the potential of bursting any time and go out of control in the near future.

SECTION B: TRENDS AND PATTERNS OF POPULATION CHANGE IN J&K

7

Population Changes in J&K : 1991

1. Population Growth

[i] Population change represents a continuing phenomenon in all societies of the world irrespective of their differences in region, religion, culture, literacy, economy, polity, and social structure. Equally important stands the fact that population changes have effected all sectors and sections of society. As a result of this situation, while composition of many societies was changed partly or wholly, different fertility and mortality rates gave rise to different types of population growth rates. Like in other societies in the world, population changes have also occurred in J&K state in the 20th century, especially in last six decades. A wholistic view of population changes in J&K reflects in the following table:

Table 1. Population Growth in J&K

Year	*Total Population [in lakhs]*	*Percentage*			
		Males	*Females*	*Urban*	*Rural*
1941	29.46	53.51	46.49	86.88	13.12
1951	32.54 [estimates]	53.36	46.64	85.95	14.85
1961	35.68	53.25	46.75	83.34	16.66
1971	46.16	53.25	46.76	81.41	18.59
1981	59.87	52.84	47.16	78.95	21.83
1991	77.18 [estimates]	52.00	48.00	76.79	23.83

Source: Census of India, 1941 - 1991, New Delhi.

The precreding table shows clearly that J&K has experienced significant degree of population growth in the last six decades. While there has been an increase in population of 161.9 per cent during the last 50 years, the maximum growth rate of 29.69 per cent was recorded in the decade of 1971 - 1981. This growth rate stands higher in comparison with many developing countries and the national average in India [i.e., about 18 per cent] in the same decade. This situation of growth in population was experienced more or less in all districts. In the decade of 1971-1981, while Budgam district showed the higher growth rate of 36.11 per cent and Doda district recorded the lowest growth rate in the state, i.e., 23.88 per cent.

[ii] The above table reveals significant degree of change in the sex composition of population in the state. While the sex ratio [number of females per 1000 males] in 1941 was 869 in J&K, it changed to 892 in 1981. This upward trend in the sex ratio was prevalent in all districts.

[iii] Another aspect of the population change was recorded in the shift of traditional reural-urban composition. The statistics in the above table shows that while there has been continuous increase in the urban population, there has also been consistent decline in the rural population. In 1941, the rural-urban composition in J&K was 86.88 per cent and 13.12 per cent respectively, this composition stood at 76 per cent and 24 per cent respectively in the year 1991. It follows that this decrease/ increase in population share has been experienced in all districts and tehsils. It was primarily because of large scale migration from rural to urban areas in the period after 1947 due to urbanisation, industrialisation and other processes of modernisation.

2. Change in Density of Population

[i] In the broader demographic change in J&K, the aspect of density has also experienced in all areas in the state. This is very clear from the following details:

Year	Density [persons per sq. km. area]
1971	54
1981	59
1991	79

Other relevant details reveal that in 1981 and 1991, Srinagar district had the highest density of 318 and 401 persons respectively in the state. This was followed by Jammu district which had 305 and 390 persons respectively in the year of 1981 and 1991. On the other hand, the lowest density existed in the Leh district of Ladakh region and it was one person and two persons respectively in 1981 and 1991.

3. Change in Birth and Death Rates

[i] The birth and death rates have direct impact on the growth of population. It has also been experienced in the state of J&K during the previous decades. The actuality of birth and death rates in J&K are recorded in the table which follows:

Table 2. Annual Birth and Death Rates in J&K

Year	*Birth Rate*	*Death Rate*	*Gap between the two*
1970	21.95	07.87	14.00
1971	21.44	07.19	14.25
1972	31.70	10.80	20.00
1973	32.50	10.30	22.20
1974	29.50	10.10	19.40
1975	31.90	12.70	19.20
1977	31.60	11.30	20.20
1978	31.80	11.70	20.10
1979	31.10	09.30	21.50
1980	31.30	09.60	21.70
1981	31.80	09.00	22.80
1984	33.50	10.10	23.40
1986	33.40	09.00	24.40
1987	30.40	08.00	22.40
1989	31.10	07.60	22.50
1990	31.40	07.90	23.50

The above table about birth and death rates in J&K from 1970 to 1990 indicates the increasing birth rates, decreasing death rates and a widening gap between the two rates. Although the birth rate was comparatively lower in the state, the death rates have also I shown relative improvements. Both these demographic developments were due to different factors like improvement in health conditions. But, at the same time, the widening gap between two rates need to be controlled effecitively and immediately.

4. Change in Religious Composition in Population

[i] The religious composition of population in J&K is noted in the following table:

Table 3. Religious Composition of Population in J&K

Year	*Percentage*				
	Muslims	*Hindus*	*Sikhs*	*Bhuddists*	*Others*
1961	68.29	28.45	1.77	1.38	0.11
1971	65.85	28.41	2.29	1.29	0.17
1981	64.29	32.24	2.23	2.23	0.16
1991	62.34	33.50	0.00	0.00	0.00

Source: Digest of Statistics, J&K Government, 1991-92.

This table clearly reveals that there has been a continuous decrease in the Muslim population and a simultaneous increase in the Hindu population in J&K. During the period 1961 - 1991, while the Muslim proportion in total population reduced from 68 per cent to 62 per cent, the Hindu population increased from 28 per cent to 34 per cent during the same period. This had a direct impact on the majority character of Muslims in the J&K state. It is interesting to note that the continuous increase in the proportion of Hindu population was experienced in the Jammu region only. However, other minority communities had insignificant increase in their population proportion during threse six decades.

[ii] It seems important to note that an impression has grown in Kashmir that the continuous decrease in Muslim proportion of total population stood manipulated by the central government in order to change the demographic composition in the state. This argument got some degree of credibility when the Chief Minister of J&K, Dr Farooq Abdullah, made a statement that the census data has been manipulated against Muslims by the concerned agencies. [for details, see 'Kashmir Times', Jammu, Ist November 1998].

5. **Changes in Levels of Literacy**

[i] The literacy changes in J&K reveals in the following table:

Table 4. Changes in Literacy Rate in J&K

Year	*Percentage*		
	Total	*Male*	*Female*
1961	11.83	16.97	04.26
1971	18.58	28.75	09.20
1981	26.67	36.29	15.88

The table shows very insignificant percentage of 26.76 of the total population in the state in 1981. The condition of females was pathetic as they had only 15.88 per cent literacy in the same year. It is interesting to note that the poor literacy rates prevailed in the state despite the fact that education from primary to university was made free by the state government from as early as 1952. It follows that majority of the people in the state have not taken full benefit of free education provided in the government schools.

6. **Change in Marital Status**

[i] The following table gives full information about the marital status in the state:

Table 5. Marital Status of the Population, 1981

Age Group	*Percentage of Married*		*Percentage of Divorcee*	
Years	*Male*	*Female*	*Male*	*Female*
00-14	08.19	08.47	08.09	39.77
15-24	09.52	22.36	11.22	18.89
25-34	28.02	32.04	29.19	13.56
35-44	26.34	23.39	27.80	11.83
45-54	18.79	13.80	17.48	08.34
55-64	10.35	05.32	08.72	04.93
65 +	06.59	02.13	05.30	03.68

The above table reveals that while dominant married groups [i.e., 28. 02 per cent and 32.04 per cent] for males and females are respectively in the age group of 25 - 34 years, the least married group [i.e., 06. 59 per cent and 2.13 per cent] for males and females respectively belonged to the eldest age group of 65 + years Rest of the age groups belonged to medium percentages.

Same was the case of divocees [males as well as females] in this Table While the dominant group belonged to 25-34 years age groups, the least numbered groups belonged to 65 + age group.

8

Changing Religious Composition in Population in J&K: 1991

The discipline of Demography refers to study the phenomena related to human population such as its composition, birth, death, marriage and migration. As happened in the broader human society, the population also underwent deeper and wider transformation due to various factoRs The Kashmiri society too has faced micro-level as well as macro-level changes in its population in the recent past. Some of these changes are natural, caused due to population dynamics and some are imposed or manipulated by interested parties due to various reasons. However, there prevailed a serious feeling among the educated in Kashmir that population figures shown in the census reports were not correct but were manipulated by interested parties in the government.

After 1981 census figures were released in J&K, they showed a strong reaction against these [figures] and held that these were manipulated consciously. The Kashmiri intelligentsia demanded that a fresh and genuine census must be carried out. It was in that context that the then J&K government had ordered for a mid-decade census to be carried out afresh. But, the results of that census could not be made public due to political disturbances in the state at that time and stiff resistance of the non-local bureaucrats in J&K government.

These doubts about census reports in J&K were not baseless. In fact, the Kashmiri intelligentsia was aware about the plans of many political leaders, bureaucrats, professionals and businessmen to change the existing composition of population in J&K, which at present was a Muslim majority state. The Bhartiya Janata Party - BJP, an extremist Hindu nationalist political party, position on abrogation of article 370 from the Indian constitution and subsequently change the population composition in J&K was glaringly clear in its declared 'Kashmir policy'. This party had not hesitated even to take and accept the advice of the Israeli government and political and non-political leaders of that country in this regard. At the time of his visit to India, Israeli Foreign Minister, Shemon Peres, gave then clear ideas for carrying out this plan to change the dominant Muslim character of the J&K state. At the same time, some elements in other political parties in India too upheld and liked these ideas, but, they preferred to follow this objective silently. The assurances given by the ruling Congress Party leaders in this regard could not be taken for granted. The 'Babri Masjid' case stood an eye-opener in this connection.

The preceding arguments regarding heavy decrease of Muslim population in J&K are supported by census figures given in Table 1 below:

Table 1. Decrease in Muslim Population in J&K, 1951 - 1991

Year	*Total Population*	*Muslim Population*	
		Number	*Percentage*
1941	2,946,728	....	....
1951	3,253,832 [proj.]	2,277,694	70.00
1961	3,560,976	2,421,463	68.00
1971	4,616,632	3,000,810	65.00
1981	5,967,389	3,789,291	63.00
1991	7,718,700 [proj.]	4,785,594	62.00

Source: Census of India, New Delhi, 1951, 1961, 1971, 1981, 1991.

The table 1 reveals crude reality with regard to the decreasing Muslim population in J&K in the past five decades. There has been a continuous fall in the Muslim proportion in J&K and simultaneous rise in the non-Muslim proportion [especially of Hindus] in the post-1947 period. While the Muslim proportion had gone down by 8 per cent from 1951 to 1991, there had been upward trend in the Hindu proportion by about 7.50 per cent in the same period. If this trend of population continues for a few decades more, it may lead to a significant reduction in the dominant Muslim population in J&K. This may lead either to the Panjab like situation or Muslim in the state will be reduced to a minority by slight margin. On the other hand, if population of migrants from West Pakistan to Jammu in and after1947 and settled there permanently will be given the status of citizenship in the state [as they have demanded in previous decades], it will also result in significant reduction in the Muslim proportion in J&K.

It seems important as well as interesting to know that this heavy decrease in the Muslim Proportion in J&K population happened despite the fact that growth rates in the state have remained higher in comparison to average growth rates at all India level. Table 2 below clearly reveals that:

Table 2. Growth rates in India and J&K State, 1971 - 1991

Year/Decade	*Growth Rates [per 000]*	
	India	*J&K State*
1951 - 1961	21.51	29.44
1961 - 1971	24.80	29.65
1971 - 1981	24.66	29.69
1981 - 1991	23.50	28.92

Source: Census of India, New Delhi, 1951 - 1991.

The argument that Muslims in J&K state maintain higher growth rates corresponding with high birth rates and low death rates which reflect in the relevant census data but not in the final results. The census figures in Table 3 reveals clearly higher birth and lower death rates in J&K state in comparison to its national record:

Table 3. Birth and Death Rates in India and J&K State, 1971-1991

	India		*J&K State*	
Years/Decade	*Birth Rate*	*Death Rate*	*Birth Rate*	*Death Rate*
1971 - 1973	30.30	15.1	32.3	10.5
1980 - 1982	30.08	12.3	31.2	09.0
1986 - 1988	32.01	11.0	32.5	08.2

Source: Census of India, New Delhi, 1971 - 1991.

In the light of above analysis, an important question arises, i.e., whether the continuous decrease in the Muslim population in J&K State stands a 'demographic reality' or 'manipulated effort'? The Kashmiri intelligentsia believes in the latter with proper and authentic documentary support. It upheld the position that this has been done consciously under a planned effort and in a systematic way for broader political objectives.

9

Population Changes in Jammu and Kashmir: 2001

The latest census in the state of J&K was carried out in 2000- 2001. The main features of this census are as follows:

[i] The total population in the state was 10,069,917 [males 5,300,574 and females 4,769,343], while as it was 77.18 lakhs in 1991, 59.87 lakhs in 1981, 45.16 lakhs in 1971, 35.68 lakhs in 1961, 32.53 lakhs in 1951, and 29.46 lakhs in 1941. The present population in the state constituted 0.98 per cent of the national population which was 1,027,015,247 in 2001. Thus the J&K ranked 19th among 35 states and union territories of the country.

[ii] The census revealed that the decadal growth rate in the state was 30.34 per cent during 1981 - 1991 and 29.04 per cent during 1991 - 2001 respectively in comparison to the national decadal growth rates of 23.86 per cent and 21.34 per cent respectively. Thus the decadal growth in the state was higher than its national level. But, at the state level, the decadal growth has decreased, though not significantly.

[iii] The sex ratio [females per thousand males] in the population has gone in favour of females. The census revealed that the sex ratio in the state was 900 in 2001, while it was 896 in 1991. However, the sex ratio at the national level was 927 in 1991 and 933 in 2001.

[iv] The density of population in the state had also changed. While it was 77 per sq. km. in 1991, it has increased to 99 per sq. km. in 2001. In contrast, the density at the national level was 267 per sq. km. in 1991 and had increased to 324 per sq. km. in 2001.

[v] The census report revealed that there has been a phenomenal increase in the literacy of males as well as females in J&K. Accordingly, the literacy rate in the state was 54.46 per cent, males 65.75 per cent and females

41.82 per cent. However, this rate stands lower than the national literacy rate which was 65.38 per cent, males 75.85 per cent and females 54.16 per cent. It seemed that the state had made considerable progress in literacy. It was 11.83 per cent in 1961, 18.58 per cent in 1971, and 32.68 per cent in 1981. It may be mentioned here that female literacy in the state was as low as 5.05 per cent in 1961and it had jumped more than 8-fold during last 40 years. But, the state had much lower rate than the national average. According to census reports, only one district, i.e., Jammu, crossed the national average by attaining the literacy rate of 77.30 per cent, males 84.92 per cent and females 68.75 per cent. Next to Jammu is Kathua district which had recorded 65.29 per cent literacy in 2001. On the other hand, the lowest literacy rate was observed in Budgam district which was 39.54 per cent. The female literacy was as low as 26.06 per cent. Same was the situation in Kupwara district.

The official statistics provided in the preceding sections revealed that significant, basic and important changes in different population compositions were experienced in the J&K state. While total population in all regions and state at large had increased significantly, the density of population in all regions had also increased proportionately. The male-female ratio in the total population too had undergone change which has gone in favour of females quantitatively. It was because female ratio to the total population and to the males population has increased relatively. However, females ratio in the state stood much lower than the national average. It may not be out of context to mention here that the census data of 2001 released by the concerned government department had no mention of migrants staying in the state, employees of out-state origin, and the KP migrants who have left the state during last two decades.

The census data about literacy situation in the state seemed interesting. Though the overall literacy rate in the state had increased, it had not benefitted all regions equally while the Jammu region had attained higher literacy rates, Kashmir region showed comparatively poor performance. The Ladakh region had also improved significantly the rate of literacy. This situation of literacy reveals in the following table:

Table 1. Literacy Situation in J&K, 2001

S.No.	*District*	*Total Population*	*Percentage of Literacy Rate per cent*		
			Total	*Male*	*Female*
1.	Kupwara	640,013	40.80	53.55	26.83
2.	Baramulla	1,166,722	44.57	56.29	31.42
3.	Srinagar	1,238,530	59.31	68.99	48.11
4.	Budgam	593,768	39.54	51.23	26.60
5.	Pulwama	632,295	47.35	58.87	34.93
6.	Anantnag	1,170,013	44.10	55.56	31.51
7.	Leh	117,037	62.24	71.98	50.03
8.	Kargil	115,227	58.01	73.98	40.96
9.	Doda	690,474	46.92	63.56	28.35
10.	Udhampur	738,965	54.16	66.43	39.89
11.	Poonch	371,561	51.07	65.41	35.30
12.	Rajouri	478,595	57.65	69.64	44.14
13.	Jammu	1,571,911	65.29	75.73	53.92
14.	Kathua	544,206	65.29	75.73	53.92

Source: Census Records of J&K state, Srinagar, 2001.

The dismal performance of Kashmir region in the field of literacy reveals glaringly in the above table, specially in Srinagar, the summer capital and largest city in the state. Budgam and other districts in this region have also shown poor performance. This situation can be explained in terms of the long-term implications of conflict situation prevailing in Kashmir for last two decades.

10

Social Aspects of Demographic Transformation in J&K - 2011

1. Demographic Transformation: Theoretical Aspects

[i] *Demography:* Demography refers to "the scientific study of human populations, primarily with respect to their size, their structure and their development."[1] Subsequently, this word was used to study the "phenomenon connected with human population, such as births, marriages, deaths, migration and the features which influence them."[2] The other aspect of this study deals with "attempts to present future population movements."[3] Finally, demography includes a study of statistical techniques and relations existing within a population, as well as of the historical and social factoRs"[4]

[ii] *Social Demography:* It refers to a "field of study with the analysis of how social and cultural factors are related to population characteristics.[4a] Its major focus is the "impact of social and cultural factors on demographic features of society, such as patterns of marriage and childbearing, the age structure of population, life expectancy and so forth.[5] It has been argued that there are three main variables underlying population change which are fertility, mortality and migration, which are increasingly associated with factors such as age at marriage, proportion marrying, contraceptives used, all types of morbidity, rural-urban migration and so forth."[6]

[iii] *Demographic Transformation:* In the preceding context, it essentially refers to the nature, patterns, trends and features of social implications of the larger phenomenon of population changes in society. It specifically focus on broader and deeper changes in population size, structure and composition their changes and implications. In other words, it concentrates on the study of changing pattern of fertility, mortality, marriage, migration and so on. Thus the process of demographic transformation has emerged as the subject of sociologists and social demographers who have studied

mainly themes related to population changes which reflected in fertility [births], mortality [deaths] and migration [movements] trends. These themes have often been presented, treated and assessed in statistical form and are generally concerned about the contemporary era.

[iv] In this paper, the attempt will be to focus on the study of reality of social implications, qualitatively as well as quantitatively, of the process of demographic transformation as reveals in census-2011 and other relevant primary statistical sources. The sole aim will be to highlight main sociological dimensions of population change which has been experienced in J&K state in the last few decades.

[v] This paper is based mainly on the census-2011 data released by the concerned authorities so far. As is clear from its study, it is neither complete in terms of providing all necessary census details carried out in 2011 nor it covers all necessary sociological variables such as rural-urban, migration, age, sex, religion, occupation, income, culture, language, marriage, births, deaths and so on. In fact, census figures released so far have the 'partial' and 'provisional' character and these can be finalised only after some time. The demographic and sociological propositions in this paper are based on limited statistical details of census-2011. So, these propositions have to be seen and assessed in this context.

2. Increasing Population Aggregates

2.1. *Increase in Total Population:* The first important sociological feature of demographic transformation was its constant increase in total population under heads. It reflected crudely in the increase of total population in J&K which was 1,25,48,926 in 2011 in comparison to 1,01,43,700 in 2001. The district-wise and male-female details in this regard revealed in the following table:

Table 1. Increasing Population in J&K [district-wise and male-female], 2001-2011

S.No.	*District*	*Total Population*				
	2001	*2011*				*per cent of total*
		Total	*Male*	*Female*	*state*	
1.	Kupwara	650393	875564	475126	400438	06.98
2.	Budgam	607181	735773	390705	345048	05.86
3.	Baramulla	843892	1015503	422171	473332	08.09
4.	Bandipore	304886	385099	201531	183568	03.07

5.	Srinagar	1027670	1269751	675667	594084	23.56
6.	Ganderbal	217907	297003	158900	138103	02.37
7.	Pulwama	441275	570060	297988	272072	04.54
8.	Shopian	211332	265960	136303	129658	02.12
9.	Anantnag	778408	1070144	552404	517740	08.53
10.	Kulgam	394026	422786	216672	206114	03.37
11.	Leh	117232	147104	92907	54197	01.17
12.	Kargil	11907	143388	80791	62597	01.14
13.	Poonch	372613	476820	252240	224580	03.80
14.	Rajouri	483284	619266	332424	286842	04.93
15.	Kathua	511455	615711	327953	287758	04.91
16.	Doda	320256	409576	213091	196485	03.26
17.	Ramban	217944	283313	149032	134281	02.26
18.	Kishtwar	190843	231034	120496	110541	01.84
19.	Udhampur	459684	555357	298094	257263	04.43
20.	Reasi	247694	314714	166392	148322	02.51
21.	Jammu	13570777	1526406	815727	710679	12.20
22.	Samba	272539	318611	168948	149663	02.54
	Total	10143700	12548926	6665561	5883365	100.00

2.2. *Increase in Population at Province Level:* The same degree of increase in total population of three provinces of the state reflects in the following table:

Table 2. Population Increase at the Province Level, 2001-2011

S.No.	*Province*	*Total Population*				
	2001	*2011*				*per cent of*
		Total	*Male*	*Female*	*state*	*total*
1.	Kashmir province	5476970	6907623	3647466	3260157	55.03
2.	Ladakh province	236539	290492	173698	116794	02.31
3.	Jammu region	4430191	5350811	2844397	2506414	42.68

2.3. *Increasing Decadal Population Growth Rates*: The increasing trend in the total population at the state reflected also in the decadal growth rates kin percentage which have been noted below:

1.	Kupwara	34.62	12.	Kargil	20.18
2.	Budgam	21.18	13.	Poonch	27.97
3.	Baramulla	20.34	14.	Rajouri	28.14
4.	Bandipore	26.31	15.	Kathua	31.81
5.	Srinagar	23.56	16.	Doda	27.89
6.	Ganderbal	36.30	17.	Ramban	31.81
7.	Pulwama	29.18	18.	Kishtwar	21.06
8.	Shopian	25.85	19.	Udhampur	20.86
9.	Anantnag	37.48	20.	Reasi	27.06
10.	Kulgam	27.03	21.	Jammu	12.48
11.	Leh	25.48	22.	Samba	16.90

Similarly, the decadal growth rates in percentage of three provinces of the state had also increased significantly as is shown below;

[a] Kashmir province 26.12

[b] Ladakh province 18.57

[c] Jammu province 17.20

2.4. *Explanation:* The preceding statistical tables and other details clearly show overall increase in population aggregates at the state, province and district levels. While the total population at the state level has increased significantly, all three provinces have recorded impressive growth. These provinces have shown potential growth rates of 26.12 per cent, 18.57 per cent and 17.20 per cent while the state had 23.71 per cent in total. The proportion of regional population has slight change. While Kashmir and Ladakh regions maintain 55.03 per cent and 2.31 per cent respectively to state's total number, the Jammu region had 42.68 per cent of such share. The distinctive trend also reflects at the district level also. So, all districts had [comparatively] higher rates of population increase. These constantly increasing trends of population had certain usual sociological implications in three various regional societies in the state to be explained in other sections. In addition, some sociological implications has been identified by U.N. Population Fund [UNFPA] Report[7] and are applicable to this situation. The report "highlights how the world will face growing problems like finding jobs for the new army of young people, especially in poorer countries. Climate change and population growth are adding to draught and femine crisis, and manages urban sprawl as Tokyo agglomeration hits a population of 36.7 million people."[8]

3. **The Sex Ratio**

3.1. Decadal Male-Female Ratio: According to census-2011 reports, the sex ratio of population in the state [district-wise and decade-wise] for all age groups has been as is noted in the following table:

Table 3. Sex Ratio in Population in J&K, 2001-2011

S.No.	*District*	*Sex Ratio [number of females per 1,000 males]*		
		2001	*2011*	*Decadal variation*
1.	Kupwara	906	843	63
2.	Budgam	911	883	48
3.	Baramulla	905	873	32
4.	Bandipore	894	911	17
5.	Srinagar	841	879	18
6.	Ganderbal	917	869	48
7.	Pulwama	942	913	29
8.	Shopian	950	951	01
9.	Anantnag	911	937	26
10.	Kulgam	945	951	06
11.	Leh	823	583	240
12.	Kargil	837	775	62
13.	Poonch	919	890	29
14.	Rajouri	878	863	15
15.	Kathua	898	877	21
16.	Doda	913	922	09
17.	Ramban	889	901	12
18.	Kishtwar	904	917	13
19.	Udhampur	846	863	17
20.	Reasi	880	891	11

21.	Jammu	865	871	06
22.	Samba	897	886	11
	State level	872	883	09

3.2. *Sex Ratio at Province Level:* The similar-type of sex ratio revealed at the province level which reveals in the table below:

Table 4. Sex Ratio in the State at Province Level, 2001-2011

S.No.	*Province*	*Sex ratio*		
		2001	*2011*	*Decadal variation*
1.	Kashmir province	914	900	14
2.	Ladakh province	830	679	151
3.	Jammu province	888	888	00

3.3. *Explanation and Evaluation:* The above two tables clearly show the downward trend in sex ratio in all districts and provinces, despite their variety and differences in many fields of life. In this downfall, in a decade's period, while Ladakh has recorded 151 downward trend, Kashmir has experienced 14 downward trend. Jammu province has gone neither up nor down, it has maintained same figures in 2001 and 2011. Almost all districts, except some, in the state had static or downward trend. While the Leh district recorded downfall of 240 from 823 per 1,000 in 2001 to 583 per 1,000 in 2011, the Udhampur district experienced the rise of 17 decadal rate from 846 in 2001 to 863 in 2011. However, most of the districts faced absolutely downward trend, which follows this trend at the national level. The decreasing sex ratio has completely negative social impact on females and they remain unequal sex in participation in societal activities. In general, this downfall of sex ratio in J&K can be explained in terms of macro and micro level factoRs In the former case, the practice of female foeticide seems dominant and determining factor, in the latter case, the conflict situation seems the contributing factor. Other contributory factor at the local level can be identified as limitations on the part of census personnel and authorities such as no experienced staff and manipulation by authorities at the higher level. It is in this context that the professional credibility of J&K census reports has been questioned by some experts in previous few decades.[9]

4. Sex Ratio, 00-06 Years Age Group

4.1. It seems important to mention here that the census-2011 reports revealed the undesirable trend of extreme decrease in the sex ratio of 00-06 years age group. The total population in 0-6 years age group was 20.08 lakh in which 10.80 lakh were males and 09.27 lakh females. Thus the sex ratio in this age group was 859 per 1,000 in 2011. This negative trend in population in the state, especially in Kashmir province, reflects in details noted in the following table:

Table 5. Sex Ratio of Population 00-06 years Age Group, 2001-2011

S.No.	*District*	*2001*	*2011*	*percentage of total population*
1.	Kupwara	1021	854	22.50
2.	Budgam	1004	832	20.69
3.	Baramulla	961	866	15.94
4.	Bandipoore	967	893	15.66
5.	Srinagaar	928	869	12.28
6.	Ganderbal	1014	863	17.02
7.	Pulwama	1016	836	17.13
8.	Shopian	1011	883	15.14
9.	Anantnag	977	832	19.28
10.	Kulgam	1003	883	16.64
11.	Leh	955	944	08.03
12.	Kargil	980	978	14.21
13.	Poonch	959	895	17.64
14.	Rajouri	905	857	19.14
15.	Kathua	847	836	13.02
16.	Doda	959	932	17.34
17.	Ramban	968	931	19.32
18.	Kishtwar	977	922	16.83
19.	Udhampur	912	887	14.88
20.	Reasi	952	921	17.73
21.	Jammu	819	795	10.47
22.	Samba	798	788	11.93
	State	941	859	....

4.2. The above table reveals that the downward trend in the sex ratio of 0-6 age population, which comes to per cent of the total population in the state, is glaringly clear in almost all districts. The extreme downfall can primarily be related to the practice of female foeticide. It also stands higher than sex ratio at the national level, i.e., 900 per 1,000 males in 2011. Following this decreasing trend, the districts in Kashmir province have shown worst performance in sex ratio.[10] Consequently, six districts of Kashmir province compose among 10 worst performance districts in decreasing sex ratio in 0-6 years age group in 2011 in the country. This is clear from the table below:

Table 6. Least Sex Ratio [0-6 years age group] in 10 Districts in India

S.No.	*District*		*Child Sex Ratio*	*Change since 2001*
1.	Pulwama	[J&K]	836	173
2.	Budgam	[J&K]	832	170
3.	Kupwara	[J&K]	854	167
4.	Anantnag	[J&K]	831	130
5.	North District	[Sikkim]	897	98
6.	Bid	[Maharashtra]	801	93
7.	Pithoragarh	[Uttrakhand]	812	90
8.	Baramulla	[J&K]	866	83
9.	Srinagar	[J&K]	869	82
10.	Mon	[Nagaland]	900	73 [11]

4.3. The extreme downward trend in 0-6 years age group population, as reflects crudely in the above table, can be explained by general and particular factors. The general factors reflect in extreme sense the national trend of decreasing sex ratio in this particular age group. These factors can be identified as general tendency among people in the state to opt for girl abortion after detecting the female sex of the child in the womb in advance. In reality, this tendency has become common at all-India level. A WHO survey conducted recently divulged that about 66 per cent Indians use unsafe route to check the sex of the baby and subsequent operations.[12] Again, another report confirmed this by observing that rampant use of pre-natal sex determination technology in rural India has led to sharp fall in the child sex ratio [CSR] in the country in 2011.[13] In the J&K state, the number of sex determination clinics and illegal abortion shops has increased sharply and alarmingly.[14] Showing serious concern over this development, the state government forcibly closed down many such clinics and ordered a fresh survey of 0-6 age group population, especially at the time of registration of pregnancy and birth of children.[15]

4.4. The particular factors include the 'conflict situation' factor, as 8 out of 10 districts fall in the category of violence hit states. In the case of J&K, the following conflict related factors contributed to decreasing effect on child sex ratio in the state in 2011: [a] Late marriage: the conflict in Kashmir had directly contributed to the emergence of late marriage which had effected the fertility rate in all classes in the valley. A relevant study of the author revealed that while actual age of marriage for males and females was 33 and 28 years respectively, desirable age of marriage for males and females was 26 and 21 years respectively;[16] [b] Increasing number of 'never married' persons: the 2 decade old conflict gave rise to increasing number of 'never married' group in population which reflected in the trends and ratio of population. This declining proportion was confirmed by the census-2011 reports.[17]; [c] Increase in disability: there has been phenomenal growth of disabled population in the state due to armed conflict in last 21 years The last census showed about 4 per 1,000 disabled persons in J&K in comparison to the national average of 2.5 per 1,000 and 2/1000, 2.5/1000 and 3/1000 in the states of Chandigarh, Panjab and Himachal Pradesh respectively;[18] [d] High mortality rate: it was observed that constant conflict in Kashmir has contributed to higher mortality rates in the total population, which also applies to the 0-6 age group; [e] Abnormal reproductive behaviour: the extreme form of violence in Kashmir has created conditions for abnormal sex behaviour and adversely effected the reproductive health of the couples; and [f] physical and mental health problems: the continuous armed conflict led to extreme deterioration in the standards of physical and mental health of people in Kashmir. While the former reflected in unprecedented increase of cardiological, neurological and cancerous diseases in the valley, the latter revealed in tension, depression, PTSD, suicidal tendencies[19] and other psychiatric diseases among large sections of society. All this had a cumulative effect on the sex ratio in the population.[20]

4.5. The implications of this declining sex ratio in 0-6 years age group population were considered disastrous socially and demographically. It was argued that if this trend in population continues unabated, it may lead to lesser or least number and proportion for female children, which will in turn have negative consequences for women in general and in marriage market in particular. In regard to the drastic effect of imbalance in the sex ratio, especially in 0-6 years age group, we may refer to a 'social campaign ad;[21] Issued by the Department of Sociology, University of Kashmir, Srinagar which reads as follows:

This ad. posed six pertinent demographic questions to every conscious and responsible citizen regarding long-term impact of dwindling sex ratio which were

[a] Do you want least number of women and minimum sex ratio at the cost of female survival in the near future?

[b] Do you want acute shortage of females in the marriage market after some decades?

[c] Do you want heavy increase in the population groups of 'late marriage' and 'never married'?

[d] Do you want traditional practices of gender discrimination to be continued in the social order?

[e] Do you want domestic and criminal violence against women to be a perpetual social phenomenon?

[f] Do you want to carry out the murder of your girls before they land in this world? and

[g] Do you want to continue the barbarian practice of female foeticide silently?[22]

5. Increasing Literacy Rate

5.1. The census reports reveal clearly that literacy level in the state at all levels has increased. The totality of this situation reveals in the table below;

Table 7. Literacy Rates in J&K, 2001-2011

S.No.	*District*	*literacy rate*				
		2001	*2011*			
			Male	*female*	*Total*	*Dec. variation*
1.	Kupwara	43.24	77.10	54.79	66.92	23.67
2.	Budgam	42.20	68.19	46.60	57.98	15.78
3.	Baramulla	66.93	77.35	55.01	66.93	19.25
4.	Bandipora	39.01	68.41	46.24	57.82	18.81
5.	Srinagar	63.13	78.03	63.47	71.21	08.08
6.	Ganderbal	40.46	70.73	47.82	59.99	19.52
7.	Pulwama	51.87	75.41	53.81	65.00	13.13
8.	Shopian	44.67	71.87	52.77	62.49	17.82
9.	Anantnag	47.59	74.13	54.15	64.32	15.15
10.	Kulgam	44.40	70.60	49.74	60.35	15.15
11.	Leh	65.34	89.39	64.52	80.48	15.15
12.	Kargil	60.85	86.73	58.05	74.49	13.64
13.	Poonch	51.19	81.04	54.80	68.69	17.50
14.	Rajouri	57.99	78.19	57.20	68.54	10.54
15.	Kathua	64.81	81.40	64.56	73.50	08.69
16.	Doda	53.55	80.36	50.34	65.97	12.42
17.	Ramban	43.06	71.97	40.04	56.90	13.84
18.	Kishtwar	43.31	71.75	44.13	58.54	15.23
19.	Udhampur	59.32	79.93	58.22	69.90	10.57
20.	Reasi	48.72	69.93	47.55	59.42	10.69
21.	Jammu	77.56	89.77	77.41	83.98	06.42
22.	Samba	73.98	89.77	74.39	_	_
	State	55.52	78.26	58.01	68.74	13.21

5.2. *Comparison within regions/districts:* The above tables show that districts of Jammu region are ahead in literacy rates in the state, though other regions have also experienced relative progress in literacy. While the highest literacy rate was recorded in Jammu [77.56 per cent], Samba [73.98 per cent],

Kathua [64.81 per cent] districts in Jammu region, Srinagar district only achieved that level [72.37 per cent] in the Kashmir province. The lowest literacy rate in the state [i.e., 39.01 per cent] was recorded by Bandipore district Again, there were three districts from Jammu region which recorded 50.00 per cent literacy, but the Kashmir region composed seven such districts. It can be argued that Jammu region maintained higher degree of literacy than Kashmir region.[23] The census reports of 2011 reveal that the literacy rate in Jammu region was 68.79 per cent in comparison to 63.29 per cent in the Kashmir region.[24] This situation can be explained in terms of the conflict and its impact on education in Kashmir region. Other equally important factor responsible for this situation may be identified as effective utilisation and mobilisation of the educational resources and facilities in the Jammu region.

5.3 *Comparison with other states:* The statistics in the above table also reveals lower level of literacy in J&K state in comparison to other states literacy records which are mentioned below:

- Himachal Pradesh 83.78 per cent
- Panjab 76.68 per cent
- Haryana 76.64 per cent
- Delhi 86.34 per cent
- Uttrakhand 79.63 per cent[25]

It may not be out of place to mention here that J&K state had achieved the literacy of 68 per cent in comparison to the national literacy record of 78 per cent in the year 2011.

5.4. *Decadal variation:* The above table also shows decadal variation in which the Kashmir region registered variation from 08.08 [Srinagar district] to 23.67 [Kupwara district], while the Jammu region registered variation from 06.42 [Jammu district] to 17.50 [Poonch district]. Since the latter region had already higher literacy rate in 2001, it maintained that status in 2011 too.

6. Rural-urban Composition

6.1. The census 2011 reports revealed that of the total population of 1,25,48,926 persons, the rural-urban composition was as follows:

- rural areas 91,74,820 72.80 per cent
- urban areas 34,14,106 27.20 per cent

It follows that while rural population has gone down from 78.95 per cent in 1991to 75.19 in 2001 to 72,80 per cent in 2011, the urban population has gone up from 21.00per cent in 1991 to 23.78 per cent in 2001 to 27.20 per cent in 2011. Again, of the total male population of 66.65 lakh in the state, 48.09 per cent lived in rural areas, while 18.55per cent lived in urban areas. As against this, of the total 58.83 per cent lakh females, 43.25 per cent were rural inhabitants and 15.88 were urban inhabitants. Thus while the general sex ratio in the state was 833 per 1,000, it was 899 females per 1,000 males in rural areas, there were 840 females per 1,000 males in urban areas.[26]

6.2. It was observed in the census statistics that all districts in the state had recorded continuous increase in urban population in comparison to continuous decrease in rural population. Thus increasing trend in urban population exists almost in all regions and districts, though the level and percentages differ. Moreover, it was found that comparatively more expansion of urban areas took place in the Jammu region than in the Kashmir region. This may be explained because of migration at two levels. First, migration from villages to towns to cities contined after 1947. Second, heavy migration of people from Kashmir to Jammu region during and after early 1990s.

6.3. It was also revealed from census statistics that all regions and districts recorded growth and expansion in urban population and areas, more in urban than in rural context, and more in Jammu than Kashmir region. This can also be explained in terms of the impact of conflict in the latter than in the former. It seems interesting in this context that Srinagar city recorded significant urban growth despite militancy conditions. It was reported in the local media that the historic city of Srinagar stood one among 100 fastest growing urban centre worldwide according to a survey conducted and released by London-based 'City Mayers Foundation'.[27] This status was awarded to Srinagar city considering various indicators of urban growth.

7. Number of Households and Housing Amenities

7.1. The census data related to the number of households in J&K in 2011, released by the Census Department of J&K Government on 29th March 2012, showed total number of 36,03,632 houses in the state. Out of this total, 32,99,219 houses are occupied and 3,04,413 houses are lying vacant. It follows that number of households has been increased by 8,35,000 during the last decade of 2001-2011. Moreover, 64,410 vacant houses have also been added during this decade, taking the total of this category to 3,04 lakhs.[29] It is generally felt by experts that these vacant houses have emerged in large numbers in urban J&K only, i.e., the cities of Srinagar and Jammu and major towns in the state.

7.2. The census report also revealed that out of 20,15,086 households enumerated in J&K, about 6.80 lakh households are of poor type. These houses include 70,047 houses of "no exclusive room" implying that families" live, cook, eat, sleep and play in a single room". Another 4,48,767 households belong to one room type and another 5,55,267 households belong to poor category. Other households, about 7.80 lakhs, belong to category having 3, 4, or 5 rooms. About 25 per cent across the state live in kitchen or have one room in addition to the kitchen.[30]

7.3. The important inference drawn from the census statistics is that while joint family system, inhabiting two married couples, has reduced from 15.09 per cent of total families in 2001 to 13.50 per cent in 2011, that of single households increased from 70.30 per cent in 2001 to 73.53 per cent in 2011. About 9.83 per cent of households have no married couples, meaning that these were owned by divorcees or widows with or without children. The single member households have increased from 29.86 per cent to 30.16 per cent in a decade.[31]

7.4. In totality, the availability of houses and households in J&K reflects in the following relevant statistical table:

Table 8. Total Number of Houses and Households in J&K, 2001-2011

S.No.	*District Occupied 2001*	*No. of Houses 2011*	*vacant 2001*	*No. of Households 2011*	*owned 2001*	*owned 2011*	*rented 2011*	*Total 2011*	
1.	Kupwara	136168	181664	9546	7604	86655	104807	618	106777
2.	Dudgam	143977	187839	7590	10415	81346	94980	564	96106
3.	Leh	52165	54394	8470	12599	23362	19387	893	20777
4.	Kargil	38043	48144	4432	6886	16706	16646	1419	18212
5.	Punch	113203	147408	18225	14835	59644	87711	762	88878
6.	Rajouri	157937	213578	18372	20699	81850	121447	1669	124000
7.	Kathua	174111	214847	14302	18289	96154	114949	2179	117836
8.	Baramulla	267777	259475	15576	11158	153613	144033	1100	145990
9.	Bandipore	98076	4017	55995	338	56794			
10.	Srinagar	257134	262239	15471	18011	167872	163979	5180	170561
11.	Ganderbal	……..	77346	3906	42382	308	43249		
12.	Pulwama	190968	169223	9649	8533	93616	880452	459	812241
13.	Shopian	……….	80888	5541	51503	265	41947		
14.	Anantnag	317275	277733	18335	19868	158707	141060	1150	143054
15.	Kulgam	………	121130	6818	68406	404	69136		
16.	Doda	219989	1333617	32162	11049	113431	76189	1997	78620
17.	Ramban	………	89622	11644	53377	455	54206		

18.	Kistwar	....	78371	7126	43840	463	445117		
19.	Udhampur	235217	183360	28025	24833	121859	90329	2544	93562
20.	Reasi	....	107833	13309	52218	1415	54792		
21.	Jammu	464588	502609	39848	56093	296953	274859	18255	302016
22.	Samba	....	114236	11180	607161	1646	62817		
	J&K	2768552	3603632	240003	304413	1551768	19492645	44083	2015088

Source: J&K Census Department, Srinagar, 2012.

7.5. The accommodation in the households varied, as mentioned above. The statistical details in this connection are given below:

Table 9. Variety of Accommodation in the Households, 2001-2011

S. No.	*variety/variable*	*No. of Households*			
		2001		*2011*	
		[no. & percentage]		*[no. & percentage]*	
1.	Households [no.]	1551768	100	2015088	100
2.	No exclusive room	53471	03.44	70047	03.47
3.	One room	352307	22.70	448767	22.27
4.	One-member households	44833	02.88	32751	01.62
5.	Two-member households	63418	04.08	111801	05.54
6.	One married couple h.hold	1091635	70.34	1481895	73.53
7.	Two-married couple h.holds	234297	15.09	272123	13.50
8.	Access to tapped water	814366	52.47	1288451	63.94
9.	No latrine households	727166	46.86	983791	48.82
10.	Drinking waste water to open	921084	59.35	1051004	52.15

Source: Ibid.

[i] The census details divulged that, during the last one decade, though J&K received 20 lakh tourists, it has only 7,473 lodging facilities, which stands very less for a state that has a vast tourism potential.

[ii] The growth of infrastructure in the health sector has not increased/improved much during the last one decade. For a population of 1.25 crores in the state, there were only 6,278 hospitals/dispensaries. It follows that there is one hospital or dispensary for every 1,998 persons in the state in 2011.

[iii] The growth in education sector shows increase in the number of educational institutions from 12,455 in 2001 to 31,843 in 2011, i.e., 65 per cent increase.

[iv] A significant growth was observed in the places of worship in the state during 2001-2011. While the number of worship places like temples, mosques, gurduwaras and churches was 32,025 in 2001, their number has increased to 49,1355 in 2011, implying the growth of more than 53 per cent.

[v] Only 34.70 per cent of total population gets tap water at home from treated sources, while 29.00 per cent of total population have tap water facility available through untreated sources and the remaining population rely on sources like wells, hand pumps, tube wells, springs, ponds and lakes. Of 20.15 lakh households in J&K get tap water at home. There seems a trend that particular districts across the state lack access to water. Kupwara is the worst hit where 23 per cent of the households still use water from stream for drinking. The scale of untreated water supply is acute in Doda [65.30 per cent], Kulgam [62.40 per cent], Kistwar [55.20 per cent], Shopian [49.00 per cent], Kargil [48.50 per cent] and some other districts.

[vi] More than 15 per cent population continues to live their life in dark in absence of electricity facility, around 85 per cent households have power facility for lighting their houses. About 13 per cent households use primitive sources of light including kerosene lamps. 2 per cent people have no source of lighting of their houses.

[vii] While 59 per cent families use firewood to cook food and 7 per cent families use the other two means for cooking. Significant number of people use firewood, cow dung cakes and crop residue. The incidence of firewood use is higher, around 80.00 per cent, in Doda, Kistwar, Reasi, Ramban and Kupwara

[viii] Half of the households in the state do not have latrine facility at home. Of the total households, 46.10 per cent defecate in the open and 2.70 per cent use public latrines. A substantial 39.50 per cent households lack ownership to a separate bathroom and 52.20 per cent households have no drainage system in place.[32]

8. Conclusion

After explaining the sociological aspects of demographic developments in previous sections, we may formulate the proposition that societies in Kashmir, Ladakh and Jammu regions have experienced demographic and social transformation related to the phenomena of:

- Significant increase in population aggregates at all levels;
- Continuous increase in decadal population growth rates;
- Changes in male-female composition in population;
- Changes in age-group proportion in population;
- Change in literacy rates at all levels; and
- Changes in rural-urban proportion in population.

Though these demographic features do not represent all sociologically relevant and necessary variables, these essentially portray some basic and crucial aspects of demographic transformation. These aspects reveal the nature, enormity and impact of these demographic changes in the state till 2011.

At the state level, the large-scale change reflects in all regions, districts, blocks, tehsils and it had effected totality and entirety of social dynamics which resulted in conscious demographic shift that had positive and negative sociological implications. The former refers to emerging dynamic population groups, increasing population growth rate, increasing urban growth and features, and increasing literacy rates. The latter includes unequal growth rates in population in regions and districts due to various factors, socially undesirable impact of uncontrolled urban growth, trends of undesirable migration from villages to towns to cities and from Kashmir region to Jammu region, and adverse decrease in sex ratio of population, particularly in 0-6 age group. With these features, the population change in J&K had social impact which may be characterised as contextual, realistic but not productive.

References

1. United Nations, Multi-lingual Demographic Dictionary [New York, 1958].
2. S. Duncan Michell, editor, A Dictionary of Sociology [London, 1968, R,& K Paul], p. 52.
3. *Ibid.*, p.54.
4. *Ibid.*

4a. Gordon Marshell, editor, Oxford Dictionary of Sociology [New Delhi, 2006, Oxford], p. 610.

5. *Ibid.*, p. 611
6. *Ibid.*
7. The Daily Star, London [reproduced by Greater Kashmir, Srinagar, 26 October 2011.

8. *Ibid.*
9. See B.A. Dabla, "Selective Abortion of Girls in J&K", Kasheer [Srinagar], Vol. 1, 2011.
10. Based on census reports, 2011, see The Times of India [TOI] , New Delhi, 28 May 2011.
11. *Ibid.*
12. See TOI, 20 January 2012.
13. See *Ibid.*, 17 July 2011.
14. See GK, 26 April 2011.
15. *Ibid.*
16. See author's study report about "Emergence of Late Marriage in Kashmir", 2008.
17. See author's paper on Increase in 'never Married' in J&K, 2009.
18. See B. A. Dabla, "Increasing Disability in J&K", In Sociological Papers on Kashmir, Vol. II [Srinagar, 2009, J K Books].
19. See author's forthcoming book entitled Increasing Suicides in Kashmir.
20. See B.A. Dabla, "Sex Ratio and Conflict", Rising Kashmir [RK], Srinagar.
21. See RK, 2011 and Aftaab, Srinagar, 2011.
22. *Ibid.*
23. GK, 8 April 2011.
24. Based on census reports, 2011. See Kashmir Life [KL], 10 April 2011.
25. Based on census reports, 2011 See GK, 8 April 2011.
26. Based on census reports,2011, See KL 10 April 2011.
27. See GK, 2011.
28. See GK, 17 November 2011
29. See details in GK, 29TH March 2011.
30. See *Ibid.*
31. See *Ibid.* and Kashmir Life [KL], Srinagar, April 01, 2012.
32. See *Ibid.*
33. See *Ibid.*

11

Decreasing Sex Ratio in J&K: 2011

1. The National Scene

The release of provisional population growth and sex-ratio figures of 2011 census recently gave rise to serious concern about these changes in J&K state. The serious concern was shown because of three main factors:

[i] Decreasing sex ratio [females per 1000 males in population] in J&K was more than the national average and more than the previous records in 2001, 1991 and 1981;

[ii] highly decreasing sex ratio in comparison to most states in India, even backward states such as Bihar and Jharkand; and

[iii] six out of ten districts of Kashmir region in the state emerged among 10 worst-performing districts in the country related to sex ratio.

This demographic shift also debased two crucial and widely accepted social propositions that:

[i] the formal adoption and implementation of relevant social legislation/policy necessarily leads to desired and complete social transformation in actuality needed in this regard; and

[ii] the adoption and increase of modern education will create desired consciousness against the practice of female foeticide [ff] in the broader society.

In fact, the present population changes have revealed that tradition-supported and deep-rooted bias and prejudice against the female sex stands very strong. These attitudes provide the continuing life to the age-old practices of gender differentiation and gender discrimination.

2. Findings of Various Population Studies

[i] These facts about population change in India were observed even before the release of these census figures in 2011. It may be mentioned here that the downward trend in sex ratio was noticed in the earlier population studies. A recent online study published in The Larnet [May 24, 2011], based on assessment of sex ratios by birth in 0.25 million births in 3 rounds of the N. F.H. Survey data concerning the period 1990-2005, indicated that selective abortion of girls, especially for pregnancies after a first-born girl, had increased tremendously. [See Frontline, July 1, 2011] This national level survey had conveyed the following findings in categorical terms:

[a] there was a sharp decline in the girl-to-boy sex for second order births when the first born was a girl. It means that the sex ratio in the second order births was skewed, implying that selective abortion of girls was rampant; and

[b] the selective abortion was between 4.2 and 12.10 million from 1980 to 2010, with a high rate of income observed in the 1990s than in 2000;

[c] the study cautioned that the selective abortion of first-order girls might increase if fertility levels dropped further in urban areas. Most of the people lived in the states where selective abortion of girls was common and uncontrolled; and

[d] the study concluded that preference varied little by education or income but selective abortions were more common among educated and rich households. It was supported by the census figures. During the period 2001-2011 census, greater than 950 girls per 1,000 boys fell from 260 to 155 districts in the country. Of the 568 districts, 405 showed a decline in the CSR and 278 showed declining higher than the national average of 1.4 per cent. As many as 158 districts have not shown any decrease or increase. *[Ibid]*

[ii] In another multi-authors national level study, carried out by investigators and social scientists representing Centre for Global Health Research, International Institute of Population Studies, Mumbai and Institute of Medical Research and Education, Chandigarh, and other international institutes showed that selective abortion of girls had gone up in last 2 decades and accounted for much of the imbalance in the 0 - 6 years age group. [See *Ibid.*]

[iii] The census 2011 figures showed that the number of girls was 7.1 million fewer than the number of boys in the age group of 0 - 6 years, where as the number of girls was 6 million fewer than the previous census period. Taking in to consideration the yardstick of developed countries, boys out number girls slightly at birth, and global sex ratio in rich countries was between 950 - 975 girls to 1000 boys. The Indian figures showed worst and staggering standards.

2. Demographic Features of J&K : 2011

[i] First, the provisional census figures revealed the total population of J&K in 2011 was 1,25,48,926 in comparison to 1,01,43,700 in 2001. While the Kashmir region had 69,07,623 persons [55 .03 per cent of the total], Jammu region had 53,50,811 [42.68 per cent of the total], and the Ladakh region had 2,90,492 persons [2.31 per cent of the total] in the year 2011. It follows that while the decadel growth rate of Kashmir region 26.12 per cent Jammu region had 17.20 per cent and Ladakh region had 18.57 per cent The male-female proportion in 2011 was as follows:

Province	*Males*	*Females*
Kashmir	36,47,466	32,60,157
Jammu	28,44,397	25,06,414
Ladakh	1,73,693	1,16,794

[ii] The second important feature was the literacy improvement in the state which follows:

Year	*Percentage*		
	Total	*Male*	*Female*
2001	55.52 per cent	66.60 per cent	43.00 per cent
2011	68.74 per cent	78.26 per cent	58.01 per cent

The census reports revealed that there was overall increase in literacy level which reflects in the decadal variation of 13.21 per cent. While the highest literacy rate in the state was recorded in Jammu district, i.e., 83.98 per cent, the lowest literacy rate was observed in Ramban district, i.e., 56.90 per cent higher literacy districts were Leh [80.48 per cent], Kathua other [73.50 per cent] and Srinagar [71.21 per cent].

[iii] The sex ratio of the population in J&K in 2011 was as mentioned below:

[a] Kashmir province 906

[b] Jammu province888

[c] Ladakh Province 679

It was also reported that decadal variation in sex ratio stood at -82, while the net deficit was -146 at the state level. The most undesirable trend of decrease in sex ratio was observed in the Kashmir province and details are mentioned below:

District	*2001*	*2011*
Kupwara	1021	854
Budgam	1004	832
Baramulla	961	866
Bandipora	967	893
Srinagar	928	869
Ganderbal	1014	863
Pulwama	1046	836
Shopian	1011	883
Anantnag	977	832
Kulgam	1003	882
Total	993	861

Thus all districts of Kashmir province faced downward trend in sex ratio and decadal variation from 59 in Srinagar district to 210 in Pulwama. This trend revealed some features [of this trend] at the national level. This trend may be explained by macro and micro level factoRs While in the former case, the practice of femal foeticide seemed a basic factor, the conflict-related factors also seemed to have contributed to the population development. Regarding the first set of factors, it may be mentioned that people in J&K have opted for abortions after detecting the sex of child before their birth inside as well as outside the state. In the latter case, the conflict-related factors were explained as follows:

[a] The conflict in Kashmir had directly contributed to the rise of late marriage, which had affected fertility trends in all classes and groups. A relevant study of the author revealed that while the actual age of marriage

for males and females was 33 and 28 years respectively, desirable age of marriage for males and females was 26 and 21 years respectively.

[b] The two-decades long conflict in Kashmir gave rise to increasing number of 'never married' people which also reflected in the census reports, especially in 2001.

[c] There has been phenomenal growth of disabled population in J&K due to armed conflict during more than two decades. The last census records showed about 4 per 1000 population in J&K in comparison to the disability level at the national level, i.e., 2.5 per 1000 population. It also stood higher in comparison to the state disability levels of 2 per 1000, 2.5 per 1000 and 3 per 1000 in Chandigarh, Panjab and Himachal Pradesh.

[d] It was observed that constant conflict in Kashmir had necessarily contributed to higher mortality rates in different segments and sections of society.

[e] The processes of militancy and militarisation in J&K had contributed to the abnormal sex behaviour and errotic reproductive health of married couples.

[f] The 23 years long armed conflict situation in Kashmir had directly given rise to extreme deterioration in physical and mental health of general people. While the former revealed in the unprecedented increase of cardiological, neurological and cancer-related dreaded diseases in the valley, the latter was reflected in mass level tension, stressed, anxiety, PTSD, trauma, suicidal tendency and other psychiatry diseases.

Other contributory factors to heavy decrease in sex ratio in population may be identified as limitatios and mistakes in training operations and processing of census data in field and office in the state of J&K. It seems important to note here that the latest census figures have to be seen in totality of figures about all 27 variables which lead to factor analysis, inverse relationship and socio-economic analysis. The last was related with the credibility of J&K census. Since no formal agreement about sex ratio in population in the J&K has been reached so far, there seemed to credibility for its reports.

3. Extreme Decline in Sex Ratio in J&K

[i] The national level studies revealed clearly that extreme downward trend in the sex ratio was on increase and that was confirmed in the 2011 census figures. It follows that this trend prevailed in most of the states.

But, the J& K emerged as the worst performer state. It was because six out of 10 worst performing districts [related to sex ratio] were from the Kashmir province of the state. The details in this regard follows;

	District /State	*C.S.R.*	*Change since 2001*
1.	Pulwama, J&K	836	-173
2.	Budgam, J&K	832	-170
3.	Kupwara J&K	854	-167
4.	Anantnag, J&K	831	-130
5.	North District, Sikkim	897	- 98
6.	Bid, Maharashtra	801	- 93
7.	Pithoragarh, Uttarakhand	812	- 90
8.	Baramulla, J&K	866	- 83
9.	Srinagar, J&K	869	- 82
10.	Mon, Nagaland	900	- 73

[ii] It follows that J&K state, particularly the Kashmir province, has emerged as the worst-ever performer in relation to the sex ratio in population in 2011. It may be explained in terms of [i] common and easily available sex determination tests in all areas; and [ii] common and easily available selective abortion of girls.

[iii] It has been reported that there are thousands of illegal and unlicensed clinics which are involved in this heinous and criminal practice in urban as well as rural areas. The state government, especially the concerned department, have not taken this population debacle or disaster with as seriousness as it deserves. It has treated it in if *baat aiee aur giee*. Its response to this problem can be explained three specific points which follow;

First, the entire response of the government towards decreasing sex ratio revolved around the sole argument related to the practice of female foeticide. This factor can never be ignored, it must not reduce the importance of other concerned factors.

Second, first among other factors is nature of limitations in the operational methodology evolved during registering/recording and calculating the relevant data from different sources and its manipulation subsequently. It was essentially in this context of these potential doubts of the local authorities about census operations that the health department in the state ordered new census or survey of the sex ratio by the BMOs and their staff. But, so far, no interim or final report/information has been revealed in this regard. In reality, some demographers and health experts from outside the state had mentioned about methodological limitation of census operations in 2011 and earlier.

Third, this particular response reveals government's ignorance about this large number of sex detection clinics and its laxity in checking the abortions in this field. Of courset has closed down many such clinics but their number is in hundreds only and the rest must be carrying out this heinous trade without any threat. Moreover, the closure of these clinics will lead to the worsening chronic unemployment problem of the youth in J&K.

4. **The Social Dimension**

[i] The entire focus on female foetus and sex determination test clinics must not hide the social dimension of this crucial problem. The NFHS study also stressed on this aspect of stressing the change of mind-set of people at large, especially of educated, urban and upper class people in the country, in order to deal with this problem effectively. It follows that the government, its organisations, agencies and institutions must start a systematic and organised campaign against inhuman practice of selective abortion of girls.

[ii] In this regard, the social campaign sponsored by the Department of Sociology of University of Kashmir can provide inspiration. Accordingly, a social campaign was started through newspaper ads. regarding ban on sex determination tests and selective abortion of girls in Kashmir. Those who violate the law must be strictly punished. The ad. characterised the decreasing sex ratio as the "Census Alarm" and identified the dangerous consequences of this population change. It posed six pertinent demographic questions to every conscious and responsible citizen regarding the implications of change in sex ratio. These questions are:

[a] Do you want least number of women and minimum sex ratio at the cost of female survival in the near future?

[b] Do you want acute shortage of females in the marriage market after some decades?

[c] Do you want heavy increase in the population groups of 'late marriage' and 'no marriage'?

[d] Do you want traditional practices of gender discrimination to be continued in the social order?

[e] Do you want domestic and criminal violence against women to be a perpetual social phenomenon?

[f] Do you want to carry out the murder of your girls before they land in this world? And

[g] Do you want to continue the barbarian practice of female foeticide silently?

[iii] The experts also feel that the only alternative left is to legally ban the sex determination tests and selective abortion of girls and, subsequently, the government, in cooperation and collaboration of civil society, must carry out serious and continuous efforts to change the attitude and mind-set of the people at large. Every individual, family and group must be involved in this sacred human cause.

SECTION C : SOCIOLOGICAL IMPLICATIONS OF DEMOGRAPHIC CHANGE IN J&K

12

Disability and its Rehabilitation in J&K

1. Disability - Meaning and Definition

[i] New Oxford Dictionary explains it in terms of the people with a permanent illness or injury that makes it difficult to them to move part of their body completely and easily. It essentially implies loss or lack of functioning, physical or mental, which unlike illness is usually permanent. It has been classified in five major types which are disability in [a] seeing, [b] speech, [c] hearing, [d] movement, and [e] mental.[1]

[ii] Halender, an eminent expert, suggests that disability may be defined as follows:

"A disabled person is one who in his/her society is regarded or officially recognised as such because of a difference in appearance and/or behaviour, in combination with functional limitation or activity restriction."[2]

[iii] On the other hand, World Health Organisation [WHO] has provided definition of disability and other inter-changeable terms as follows:

[a] Impairment: Any loss or abnormality of psychological, physiological or anatomical structure or function;

[b] Disability: Any restriction or lack resulting from impairment of ability to perform an activity in the manner or within the range considered normal for a human being; and

[c] Handicap: A disadvantage for a given individual, resulting from an impairment or disability, that limits or prevents the fulfillments of a role that is normal, depending on age, sex, social and cultural factors, for that individual.[3]

Two more terms have been explained in relation to the concept of disability which are:

[a] *Prevention:* It means measures aimed at preventing the onset of mental, physical or sensory impairments or at preventing impairment, when it has occurred, from having negative physical, psychological and social consequences.[4]

[b] *Rehabilitation:* A goal-oriented and time-limited process aimed at enabling an impaired person to reach on optimum mental, physical and social functional level, thus providing him with tools to change his own life. It can involve measures intended to compensate for a loss of function or functional limitation and other measures intended to facilitate social adjustment or readjustment.[5]

[iv] In brief, a person with disability, according to the 'Person with Disability Act, 1995' is a person suffering from not less than 40 per cent of any disability in the fields of [a] blindness [b] low vision [c] leprosy-cured [d] hearing impairment [e] locomotor retardation, and [f] mental illness.[6]

[v] It has generally been observed that while prejudices and discrimination are practised against disabled worldwide, they face social antagonism and social segregation on the part of broader society. Moreover, the related social taboos determine the social orientation and social treatment towards the disabled. This negative social response has proved more damaging than the physical fatality. The cultural barriers also become an obstacle in the integration and full participation of disabled persons [DPs] in all fields of life. The problem is made further complex by the fact that huge majority of DPs are usually poor people.[7]

[vi] Disability in most countries is understood as physical difference from the normal population, more in terms of medical deformity. Thus, a person could be either blind or deaf or dumb. But, this is in actuality based on subjective meaning of the term. Another view about disability emphasises it as a social phenomenon, something that is politically constructed. Thus it emerges as a result of oppressive socialisation of a given form of physiological impairment. In this way, disability becomes a "general category, which refers to the situation of those facing a barrier to normal functioning because of socio-economic and cultural constraints of hegemonic normalcy."[7-A]

2. Number and Types of Disabled

[i] According to a United Nations [UN] estimate, the total number of DPs in the world in 1990 was 500 million, which were expected to increase to 600 million by 2000 that amounts to one person inonemy ten [08]

Halender estimates of an average of 8.5 million DPs are added to this total every year or 23,000 a day. By 2025, the number will rise to 435 million in developing countries and to 138 million in developed countries. Thus the total number will be 573 million or 8.2 per cent of the world's total population.[8] The estimates about various types of disability were as follows:

[a]	movement disability	2.5 per cent to 3.0 per cent
[b]	seeing disability	0.5 per cent to 1.0 per cent
[c]	hearing disability	0.5 per cent to 1.0 per cent
[d]	learning disability	0.2 per cent to 0.4 per cent
[e]	fits disability	0.3 per cent to 0.6 per cent
[f]	psychiatric disability	0.1 per cent to 0.2 per cent
[g]	feeling [hands and feet] disability	0.1 per cent to 0.2 per cent
[h]	combination of disabilities	0.2 per cent to 0.3 per cent[9]

3. **Disability in India**

[i] Like other societies in the world, the Indian society compose a significant number of DPs which maintain a significant percentage to the world's total disabled population. It has been estimated that the rate of disability in India constitutes 1.9 per cent of the world's total population covering visual, hearing, speech and locomotor disabilities and their basic needs for social-physical security, individual respect-dignity and meaningful role-employment remains unmet.[10] It has been observed that usually the social and cultural dimensions of disability in India have proved more damaging.

[ii] The total population of disabled in India, according to 2001 census, reveals in the following table:

Table 1. Disability and its Rehabilitation in J&K

Total disabled population		21,906,769	2.10 per cent
Disability rate [per lakh population]		2,130	....
Types of disability:	seeing	10,634,881	1.00 per cent
	Speech	1, 640,868	0.20 per cent
	Hearing	1,261,722	0.10 per cent
	Movement	6,105,477	0.60 per cent
	Mental	2,263,821	0.20 per cent[11]

[iii] The proportion of disabled population in the total population of country is shown in the table below:

Table 2

Total Population	*[no. & percentage]*		*Disabled Population*
Total	*Number*	*percentage*	*percentage*
Total	1,028,610,328	100.00	2.10
Male	532,156,772	51.70	57.64
Female	496,453,556	48.26	42.46
Rural	742,490,639	72.20	74.81
Urban	286,119,689	27.80	25.19[12]

[iv] In terms of varying types, the disability in India had the following categorisation:

Table 3. Types of Disabilities in India, 2001

Type of Disability	*Number*	*percentage*	*Male [per cent]*	*Female [per cent]*
Total	21,906,769	100.00	57.54	42.46
Seeing	10,634,881	48.55	53.90	46.10
Speech	1,640,868	07.49	57.41	42.59
Hearing	1,261,722	05.76	53.40	46.60
Movement	6,105,477	27.87	63.92	36.08
Mental	2,263,821	10.33	59.84	40.16[13]

[v] The disabled population in India had the following literacy rates:

Table 4. Literacy Rates among Disabled in India, 2001

Total	*Persons [per cent]*	*Males [per cent]*	*Females [per cent]*
Total	49.31	58.15	37.32
Rural	44.40	54.11	31.31
Urban	63.87	70.05	55.36[14]

4. Disability Legislation in India

[i] In order to take full care of Disability in India, a comprehensive legislation was passed in the parliament in 1995 in the name of "Persons with

Disabilities [Equal Opportunities, Protection of Rights and Full Participation] Act - 1995". The two major objectives of this Act were

[a] promoting and ensuring equality and full participation of persons with disabilities; and

[b] protecting and promoting their economic and social rights.[15]

On the whole, the Act was oriented to the fulfillment of following objectives:

[a] to spell out the responsibility of the State towards the prevention of disabilities, protection of rights, provision for medical care, education, training, employment and rehabilitation of persons with disabilities;

[b] to create barrier-free environment for persons with disabilities;

[c] to remove any discrimination against persons with disabilities in sharing the development benefits, vis-à-vis non-disabled persons;

[d] to counteract any situation of the abuse and of exploitation of persons with disabilities;

[e] to lay down strategies for comprehensive development of programmes and services and equalisation of opportunities for persons with disabilities; and

[f] to make special provision for the integration of persons with disabilities into the social mainstream.[16]

This important legislation was passed in consideration of various problems faced by the disabled such as employers prejudiced view against DPs and their ability to look after work, DPs as economic liability and have potential, social stigmatisation, discrimination, transport problems, and access to public facilities and buildings.[17]

5. Disability in J&K

[i] The J&K state faces the problem of disability in acute form. In fact, its occurrence in the state has reached to the alarming level and it maintains the proportion which is higher than the disability at the national level. According to 2001 census records of J&K [2011 census reports about disability not released so far], the state had following number of disabled persons:

Table 5

S.No.	*Persons/Sex*	*Total*	*Rural*	*Urban*
1.	Persons	302,670	229,718	72,952
2.	Males	171,816	129,443	42,373
3.	Females	130,853	100,275	30,579[18]

The figures of disability in the state in 2011, according to experts, must have doubled. The reasons cited for the high increase include [i] more than the normal increase due to hilly nature of the state, and [ii] higher rate of disability due to armed conflict in last two decades. Thus an estimated/ calculated account of disabled persons in the state revealed 605,340 persons [males 343,632 and females 251,708].

According to 2001 census statistics, five major types of disability prevailed in the state and their numbers were as follows:

Table 6

	Type of disability	*Total*	*Males*	*Females*
1.	Disability in seeing	208,713	116,034	92,679
2.	Disability in speech	16,956	9,748	7,208
3.	Disability in hearing	14,157	7,693	6,464
4.	Disability in movement	37,965	23,312	14,653
5.	Mental disability	24,879	15,029	9,850[19]

The above figures show that blind, movement and mental disability were more prevalent in proportion than speech and hearing disability. This may be explained by factors of hilly topography and militancy character of the state.

It was revealed in the census figures that majority of the disabled [i.e., about 56 per cent of the total] were illiterate in comparison to a minority of literates [i.e., about 44 per cent of the total] in the year 2001.[20] Again, while majority of disabled belonged to lower and middle classes, minority of them were from upper classes and elites.

A comparative view of the relevant data released by census 2001 revealed that higher rates of disability in J&K state in comparison with the national average and north Indian states' rates. Thus while the national level disability percentage in 2001 was 2.12 per cent [males 2.36 per cent and females 1.87 per cent], the J&K state had 3.00 per cent [males 3.24

per cent and females 2.74 per cent]. The north Indian states of Panjab, Himachal Pradesh and Chandigarh [which share the hilly character with J&K] had disability rates of 1.74 per cent, 2.56 per cent and 1.72 per cent respectively in the same year.[22] It follows that J&K state had the highest rate of disability [i.e., 3.00 per cent] in the whole country which can be explained in terms of the hilly topography of the state and continuing armed conflict situation in last 23 years

The highest rate of disability in J&K reflects in district-level rates which are mentioned below:

[i]	Kupwara	3.25 per cent	[ii]	Baramulla	3.86 per cent
[iii]	Srinagar	2.81 per cent	[iv]	Budgam	2.58 per cent
[v]	Pulwama	2.53 per cent	[vi]	Anantnag	2.63 per cent
[vii]	Leh	2.31 per cent	[viii]	Kargil	2.51 per cent
[ix]	Doda	3.29 per cent	[x]	Udhampur	3.00 per cent
[xi]	Poonch	3.80 per cent	[xii]	Rajouri	3.15 per cent
[xiii]	Jammu	3.02 per cent	[xiv]	Kathua	2.30 per cent[23]

The preceding statistics clearly shows that four particular frontier districts of Baramulla, Poonch, Kupwara and Rajouri had higher rates of disability against non-frontier districts in the state. This was also because of the context of armed conflict in the state during more than two decades.

The central government has responded to the problem of disability in the country positively. It has legislated the "Persons with Disability act" in 1995 which is aimed

- To spell out the responsibility of the state towards the prevention of disabilities, protection of rights, provisions of medical care, education, training, employment and rehabilitation of persons with disabilities ;
- To create barrier-free environment for persons with disabilities;
- To remove any discrimination … in sharing of development benefits;
- To counteract any situation of the abuse and exploitation of persons with disabilities;
- To lay down strategies for comprehensive development of programmes and services and equalisation of opportunities for persons with disabilities; and
- To make special provision for the integration of persons with disabilities into the social mainstream.[24]

However, the state government's response to this problem has not been so active and positive. Except emphasising implementation of the central act, its total response may be characterised as 'apathetic'. Its policy, programmes and schemes were not specifically directed to eliminate this problem in totality within a specific time frame and particular methodology. It has not accepted the gravity of this problem. In actuality, its response has proved negligent which reflected crudely in the failure of implementation of one of the important schemes about disabled persons sponsored by the central government in the state. Even the concerned government department has failed to collect basic data about disabled persons in J&K. In this context, even the Governor of the state was compelled to emphasise on the Social Work department to conduct tehsil-wise survey of disabled persons in the state.[25] There are some centrally-sponsored schemes which provide some minimum benefits to the disabled persons. But, at the same time, these are neither fully functional nor the entire disabled community has been covered. These facilities also do not have expert personnel, modern medical technology and other resources.

6. Sociological Aspects of Disability in Kashmir

[i] It is now clear that disability exists in Kashmir in its extreme form. It has all established and conventional forms/types, though mental disability among women and children exists at the extreme level. Its causative dynamics and socio-medical implications are also clear, especially in the context of conflict situation during last 23 years The data regarding disability presented in the preceding sections supports this proposition.

[ii] However, there are other important sociological dimensions which need to be emphasised here. First, disability in Kashmir was not limited to the physical and mental health of the individual, it effects the individual's social life and social relations in particular. In actuality, disability remains a physical and mental problem in the initiation and affects the individual's life only. But, it becomes a real and pathetic problem when it becomes a social problem because it affects the entirety of social life and individual becomes sociologically pathological and social environment gets depressive and degenerative. How it happens? It happens when the disabled person develops personal-social dependence and he/she gets exposed to social situations repeatedly. His/her social dependence creates a depressive

personality and develops total dependence on family and other members of society. With this reaction, one gets depressive and offensive personality traits. As a result of this interactive situation, there emerges a social reaction called "stigma" which is related to the person's identity which gets the lowest possible social value.

[iii] In order to sensitise the issue of disability at the mass level, the 22 Rehabilitation International World Congress, held in Incheon in October-November 2011, identified and advocated 10 specific goals which are

- [a] reducing poverty and enhancing work and employment prospects,
- [b] promoting participation in political processes,
- [c] enhancing access to the physical environment,
- [d] strengthening social protection,
- [e] expanding early intervention and education of children with disabilities,
- [f] ensure gender and women's empowerment,
- [g] ensuring disability-inclusive disaster risk reduction and management,
- [h] improving the reliability and comparability of disability data,
- [i] accelerating the ratification and implementation of the U.N. Convention, and
- [j] advancing sub-regional, regional and inter-regional cooperation.[26]

[iii] In the last months a local weekly newspaper, Kashmir Life, [6 October, 2012], published stories of two disabled children which revealed the pathetic and sadistic response of the larger society. These stories reflected the following sociological features of these two disabled cases and their society:

- There was complete self-consciousness, self-conditioning and internalisation of the disabled children and their both parents;
- They got socially disassociated completely and alienation became their fate;
- As a result, they developed the consciousness about stigma related to disability and also created an undesirable and un-interactive identities

and even their brothers, sisters, parents and other relatives either left them alone or never visited them or avoided them always ;

- It gave rise to their depressive and reactive personalities, in which they suffered themselves;
- They could not get proper, needed and complete medical treatment immediately or at the time when it was needed most;
- There was a common criticism of these disabled persons and this perception was encouraged by women particularly;
- These members of family and society got out of competition in the social life, they considered themselves as 'failures' or 'drop-outs';
- There emerged a social offensive against these individual in all fields of life and they were consciously discriminated and even opposed;
- The disability to these children was of inherited nature and it could have been treated at its earlier stage. But, no proper attention was paid to these;
- They developed total social dependence on family and society and were less liked and more disliked by other members;
- In general, they faced a downward trend and downward mobility in every field of life;
- No proper treatment to different disabiitieds was provided in time. It was mainly because there was no expertise and no technology available for this disease;
- Though there are positive and sympathetic responses from the society, there was also social repulsion against disabled persons;
- The former type of positive and sympathetic response led to societal efforts in a systematic and organised way through the functioning of national and international non-governmental organisations and agencies;
- Two such positive initiatives were taken by 'Chotey Tarey' and 'Shafqat chears this in m/s School'.

7. **The NGO Response**

In this background, some small efforts were initiated for the rehabilitation of disabled persons by local/national/international NGOs and other groups. This humble effort on the part of NGO sector and civil society caters the needs of particular sub-groups of disabled and its focus is on specialised areas/fields. Though these efforts are limited and time-bound, it may help the governmental efforts in this regard. It reveals the strong potential of NGO sector in responding to problem of disability in J&K.

One such organised, systematic and specialised effort has been carried out by "Shafaqat chears this word Special School for Mentally Challenged and Multiple Disabilities"[26] based in Srinagar, which the author had opportunity to visit. Founded in 1995, it provides rehabilitation, treatment, services and facilities to 150 indoor and about 500 outdoor disabled children in the fields of physiotherapy, occupational therapy, audiology, speech therapy, recreational therapy, computer and vocational training, development therapy, special education and social activities. The general/ professional services and facilities in the school are of world class in an ideal environment of rehabilitation and corrective measures for the total welfare of the disabled children.[27]

References

1. Gordon Marshall, A Dictionary of Sociology [New Delhi, 1996, Oxford].
2. Halender quoted in V.V. Krishna, B.S.V. Dutt and K.H. Rao, eds. Disabled Persons [New Delhi, 2005], p. 7.
3. See Krishna, etel., op. cit., No. 2, p. 179.
4. *Ibid.*
5. *Ibid.*, p. 180.
6. See Varinder Singh and Rachna Arora, "Disability and the Laws in India" in Awadesh Kumar Singh Rights of the Disabled [Perspectives, Legal Protection and Issues] , [New Delhi, 2008, Serials Publications], pp. 249-50.
7. See Krishna, op. cit., p. 191.

7-A. See Frontline, Chennai, January 13, 2013.

8. *Ibid.*, p. 9.
9. *Ibid.*, p. 10.
10. Saghistha and K. Madeswsaran, "Employment Opportunities for the Persons with Disability in India: Issues and Challenges" in Krishna, et el, No. 2, p. 4.
11. Krishna, *Ibid.*, p. 275.
12. Krishna, *Ibid.*, p. 276.

13. Krishna, *Ibid*, p. 278.
14. *Ibid.*
15. Singh and Arora, op. cit., No. 6, p. 252.
16. Singh, op. cit., No. 6, p. 22.
17. Saghistha and Madeswasaran, op. cit., No. 10, p. 5.
18. Government of India, Census of India, New Delhi, 2001.
19. *Ibid.*
20. *Ibid.*
21. *Ibid.*
22. *Ibid.*
23. *Ibid.*
24. See Singh, op. cit., No. 6.
25. See Greater Kashmir, Srinagar, May 2012
26. see Frontline, No. 7A.
27. See "Shafaqat Special School for Mentally Challenged and Physical Disabilities", Srinagar, 2008, J&K Medicare Society.
28. *Ibid.*

13

Rising Population of "Never Married" in J&K

1. Phenomenon of 'Never Married' in Kashmir

1. It has been observed sociologically that nature, pattern, practice and other features of marriage in the human society have been shaped by various socio-economic and other factors, in addition to natural and biological factoRs At the same time, sociological studies have revealed that all marriage practices and patterns have undergone a significant degree of change as a result of implications of processes of change and development. Like other human societies in the world, the preceding propositions can be applied equally to the Kashmiri society. Thus in an important study about marriages in the Kashmir valley, carried out by the author in 2008,[1] it revealed that 'late marriage' has emerged as a significant trend. According to this study, the average actual/desirable age of marriage for men and women was revealed as mentioned below:

(i)	Actual age of marriage	Males	31.53 years
		Females	27.87 years
(ii)	Desirable age of marriage	Males	23.63 years
		Females	20.70 years[2]

The survey identified the following major causes of late marriage;

[i]	Acute poverty	57.66	per cent
[ii]	Increasing unemployment	56.00	per cent
[iii]	Dowry in different forms	56.50	per cent
[iv]	Attainment of higher education	31.33	per cent
[v]	prevailing conflict situation	15.60	per cent[3]

The survey also showed following major consequences of late marriage;

[i]	Decrease in household population	24.33	per cent
[ii]	Mental depression	24.06	per cent
[iii]	Increase in suicide rate	19.66	per cent
[iv]	Emerging immoral activities	12.36	per cent
[v]	Pre-marital sex relations	10.46	per cent[4]

2. In the same way, in another survey about "Changing Marriage Practices in Kashmir" [report of the survey not published so far], it revealed that following practices of marriage are in vogue in the Valley at present:

[i] Monogamous marriage		89.10	per cent
[ii] Polygamous marriage		10.10	per cent
[iii] Pattern of Polygamy			
	II wife	85.56	
	III wife	07.57	
	IV wife	05.96	
[iii]	Encdogamy	45.35	per cent
	Exogamy	54.80	per cent
[iv]	Hyper-gamy	23.76	per cent
	Hypo-gamy	16.11	per cent
[v]	Patri-local	64.21	per cent
	Matri-local	07.31	per cent
	Neo-local	28.53	per cent[5]

3. Similarly, the practice of "Never Married" represents a social phenomenon which is present in all human societies, less in primitive societies and more in modern societies. In the demographic sense, it has a population dimension, i.e., it refers to a particular population group entitled as "Never Married"[6]. The composition of this group had definite implications for general population dynamics, fertility-mortality rates and marriage rates [which refers to number of married persons in the total population].[7] It has been observed that this composition affects marriage-rates in some particular groups and areas. Accordingly, while migrants have generally lower marriage-rate due to their extreme degree of mobility, the low rate also figures in areas of conflict . Thus this category of "never married" has

certain set causes and consequences. swell The perpetual armed conflict situation plays a negative role vis-à-vis marriages, i.e., it generally lowers the marriage -rate and, consequently, increase the number of "never married" persons. That has happened at different times, especially during war times, and in different places such as Bosnia and is now happening in the Indian state of Jammu and Kashmir. Though in these situations, normal demographic factors affect the composition of married people in total population, but the constant conflict and migration has proved a determining factor in this regard.

4. Though actual figures about latest situation in J&K are not available, Census statistics of 2001 is available which tells us about this situation in the preceding decade, i.e., 1990s. According to this census, total number of "never married" and "married" persons in the state in 2001 was as follows:

Table 1. Number of never-married and married persons in J&K, 2001

S.No.	*Sex*	*never-married*		*married*	
		No.	*percentage of total pop.*	*No.*	*percentage of total pop.*
1.	Persons	5,649,235	55.69	4,187,479	41.21
2.	Male	3.099,875	54.87	2,161,741	51.62
3.	Female	2,549,360	45.12	2,025,738	48.51

The distribution of these never-married and married persons in terms of age and sex was as reveals in the following table:

Table 2. Number of never-married and married persons in terms of age and sex in J&K, 2001

S.No.	*Age Group*	*never-married*		*married*	
		No.	*percentage of total pop.*	*No.*	*percentage of total pop.*
1.	00-09	2,256,366	39.94	000	00.00
2.	10-14	1,332,333	23.58	26,642	00.60
3.	15-19	1,061,859	18.79	83,313	01.98
4.	20-24	581,596	10.29	304,317	07.26
5.	25-29	243,983	04.31	538,353	12.85
6.	30-34	71,710	01.26	615,882	14.70

7.	35-39	23,089	00.40	653,636	15.60
8.	40-44	11,163	00.20	511,090	12.20
9.	45-49	6,447	00.11	432,335	10.32
10.	50-54	4,951	00.08	308,157	07.35
11.	55-59	3,153	00.05	227,027	05.42
12.	60-64	5,091	00.09	191,673	04.56
13.	65-69	3,532	00.08	119,080	02.84
14.	70-74	5,219	00.09	84,120	02.00
15.	75-79	3,204	00.05	37,084	00.88
16.	80 +	4,022	00.07	41,597	00.91

The above tables clearly reveal that there existed a huge number of 'never-married' persons in J&K, i.e., 5,649,235 in 2001. This also reveals in all age groups, especially younger and elder age groups. It seems important to note here that these figures deal with the situation in the decade of 1990s and reported in 2001. Concerned experts feel that number and proportion of never-married persons must have increased significantly in unstable and conflict-ridden valley of Kashmir. Even the number and proportion of 'never-married' persons in 2001 in J&K was higher than the national average, which can be seen in the following table:

Table 3. Number of 'never-married' persons in 2001, India and J&K

S.No.	*Census unit*	*Persons No.*	*percentage*	*Male No.*	*percentage*	*Female No.*	*percentage*
1.	India	512,667,639	49.84	289,619,359	54.42	223,048,280	44.92
2.	J&K	5,649,235	55.69	3,099,875	54.87	2,549,360	45.22

The preceding table shows clearly the difference between the proportions of 'never-married' persons at the national and state levels. While it is higher in the case of J&K, i.e., 55.69 per cent, it stands lower at the national level, i.e., 49.34 per cent. In both cases of male and female proportions, it stands higher in the state than at the national level.

5. All three tables and following population developments reveal that proportion of 'never-married' persons has increased significantly in last two decades which has dangerous implications for overall balanced growth

of population in J&K, especially the Kashmir province. While the normal demographic dynamics has led to this undesirable situation, it was equally contributed by conflict situation factor. In addition to moral, ethical, cultural and social implications, this increasing phenomenon has posed potential demographic threat to the local community. In this context, the local intelligentsia must respond to this alarming situation and must initiate the relevant efforts to restore credibility, applicability and respectability to the practice of marriage at the household and societal levels.

References

1. Report on Emergence of Late Marriage in Kashmir [2008, Department of Sociology and Social Work, University of Kashmir, Srinagar]
2. *Ibid.*
3. *Ibid.*
4. *Ibid.*
5. Survey on Changing Marriage Practices in Kashmir Valley [2009, Department of Sociology and Social Work, University of Kashmir, Srinagar], unpublished.
6. See Census of India, 2001.
7. Peter R. Cox, Demography [New Delhi, 1972, United Book Store].
8. *Ibid.*
9. See Census of India, 2001.

14

Increasing Suicides in Kashmir

1. The Kashmir Context

[i] Though we are concerned about the whole state of J&K, this study has concentrated specifically on the Kashmir region. Some propositions and some data has been presented here which deal with the state as a whole, but all necessary theoretical and statistical details about suicides have been presented about the Kashmir region only. It has been done because of four contextual reasons which are:

[a] the traditional situation in Kashmir was such which had neither ideational nor functional character or existence about suicides;

[b] this dominant situation has experienced the processes of change and development in the modernisation context, which was associated with its pathology, which gave rise to the phenomenon of committing suicide in addition to other grave social problems;

[c] in the recent past, the introduction of the armed conflict and its necessary implications over a period of two long decades exposed the Kashmiri society at large to the extreme form of pathology which increased and intensified the acts of committing suicides. This didn't happen in any other region of the state, though some other implications were unavoidable for those regions; and

[d] now, in the present context, we face a society which has experienced the higher/highest number/rates of suicide in the country. Moreover, the emerging trend and direction of these suicides is towards their increase and intensity. Thus this social phenomenon stands unparalleled and unprecedented.

2. The Statistical Estimates

[ii] It must be noted here there is no official statistics or any other record about the nature, number and rate of suicides in the present-day society

in the state. The police stations and health/medical centres have not kept records fully, properly and at all levels. Even the local print media reports, on which this study is based, has not covered 100 per cent cases of suicides in the Kashmir region in last 21 years long period. The official statistics about suicides published by National Crime Record Bureau [NCRB], Ministry of Home Affairs, Government of India, New Delhi has not given statistical information about this pathological situation in the Kashmir region. It has not shown the number or rate of suicides in this particular unit. However, the Crime Branch of Jammu and Kashmir Police, Srinagar has issued the statistics regarding various crimes in J&K state in 2009 and 2010. According to these statistics, the registered cases [in the police stations] of abetment to suicide were 312 in 2009 and 296 in 2010 which shows higher number as well as higher rate of suicides in Kashmir.[1] This trend of high rate and increasing trend was confirmed by the statistics issued by Jammu and Kashmir Police [IGP Headquarters, Srinagar] in 2011. According to this source, the overall crime situation was as grave as reveals in the following table:

Table 3.1. Registered and not registered cases of Crime in Srinagar District

Year	*Cases registered*			*Cases not registered*	
	Normal Crimes	*Militancy-related Crimes*	*Total*	*Normal crimes Crimes*	*Militancy-related*
1989	3,479	264	3,743	559	5
2000	2,752	506	3,258	241	9
2010	2,817	63	2,880	157	2

Source: J&K Police [IGP Headquarters], Srinagar.[2]

It follows from the above statistical details that the overall trend of increasing number and rate of suicides in district Srinagar and the direction of suicides is also towards the same goal. This district-level data stands symbolic and representative. So, we can infer that with the overall trend of rising crime, there is every possibility of heavy increase in the incidence of suicide in the Kashmir region.

Though these statistical figures are partial, unrepresentative and not in totality, these [figures] give the basic idea and minimum information that will enable us to know about trends and direction of suicides in the state. In this context, we can logically and realistically assume that there exists the comparatively higher rate of committing suicides in J&K state.

1. **Higher Rate of Suicide**

In the preceding context, we may validly argue the Kashmir [and some districts in and Jammu region] experienced highest number and rate of suicides. The social observers, sociologists and other experts feel that the mass media agencies portray the higher/highest number/trends of suicides and specifically focus on most negative, damaging and disastrous implications, and emphasise strongly to control this problem effectively and immediately.

2. **Report on Suicides in The Kashmir Valley**

[i] Keeping in view emerging huge number of suicides, the author carried out a micro-level sociological study for the period of one year -1999-2000 entitled Suicides in the Kashmir Valley. A brief report of that sociological study was prepared by the author which is produced here in total:

1. **Introduction**

1.1. Suicide in general means killing oneself intentionally. Sociologically, it refers to an act on the part of individual which is essentially subject to social forces. The tendency to suicide depends less on individual psychology or the physical environment and more on individual's relation to the broader society. Thus it follows that suicide primarily represents an individual action which necessarily reveals the failure of social solidarity and is indicative of the ineffectiveness of social bonds. One of the founding fathers of Sociology, Emile Durkhiem [who has produced the trend-setting sociological study on suicides in modern times], has developed the following typology of suicides:

[i] *Altruistic Suicide:* In this type of suicide, the individual is too strongly integrated into society -a society which encourages or even requires the individual to sacrifice his or her own life.

[ii] *Egoistic Suicide:* In this type of suicide, the individual is insufficiently integrated into society, and so is not subject to the collective forces that prevent suicide and experiences an isolation and detachment conducive to it.

[iii] *Anomic Suicide:* This type of suicide depends on the social regulation of the individual's desires and ambitions. Where anomie [normlessness] is heightened in society, the individualls passions, ambitions and appetites

are increased to a level where they cannot find satisfaction, so opts for suicide.

Moreover, sociologists have emphasised that one must assess the impact of social and cultural factors on the construction of suicide statistics as well as the tendency to commit suicide. A range of studies have provided some empirical support for the evidence of the impact of social factors on levels of suicide.

1.2. The number of suicides in present-day Kashmiri society has experienced a phenomenal growth in the recent years In fact, the pattern/s of committing suicide has emerged as a significant trend in Kashmir. It is partly because of sudden rise of suicides and partly because of peaceful social situation in the traditional Kashmiri society in which suicides were either totally absent or very insignificant. Thus we may argue that a significant trend of suicides has emerged in present-day Kashmir.

1.3. The phenomenon of suicide in the valley needs to be observed/ analysed in the above-mentioned sociological framework. The global-oriented sociological propositions need to be utilised in order to explain causes, consequences, nature pattern, solutions and other important features of the going-on trend of suicides. This may prove a serious academic exercise. But, there are some serious limitations which make this work very difficult, even impossible. These limitations include non-availability of relevant data from any source [governmental sources] and any professional-academic study on suicides in Kashmir. In this context, this micro-level study stands highly relevant and badly needed. This study is an attempt to identify and explain major sociological features of the acts of suicides in Kashmir during the period of last one year.

1.4. The suicides in Kashmir may be observed in the broader context of total societal dynamics. Thus these may not be explained/analysed in relation to the development of militancy alone, but will be seen and co-related in the totality of social, cultural, economic, psychological, political, educational, demographic and other relevant factoRs It follows that while basic societal factors have determined the occurrence of suicides; the militancy-related developments have accelerated and intensified the rate of suicide in Kashmir.

2. Methodology

2.1. It has been mentioned in the preceding section too that though there has been phenomenal growth inthe suicides [with the concomitant social consciousness] in Kashmir, no minor or major study/survey has been carried out by the concerned experts. It is partly because of academic apathy towards the scientific study of this problem and partly because of non-availability of information/data and other source material on this problem. In this situation, the only source which provides some basic, but raw, information is the local press in Kashmir. The local newspapers publish daily the reports about suicides and give details about sex, age, area, cause, method, reaction of the people and so on. In the prevailing situation, this content study, which stands as one of the credible methods for scientific investigation of human behaviour, is based on the news items about suicides published in the local newspapeRs Though with certain inherent limitations, this method proved relevant and meaningful in our case.

2.2. In this content study, the scientific investigations of news-reports was carried out during the period of one year, i.e., from September 1999 to August 2000. The total cases of suicide reported in 'the local press during this period was 185. The month- wise details about suicide have been given ahead in the table 1 newspapers which were studied for knowing about cases of suicide were as follows:

[i] Greater Kashmir [English daily] Srinagar:

[ii] Srinagar Times [Urdu daily] Srinagar; and

[iii] Aftab [Urdu daily] Srinagar.

2.3. Keeping in view broader sociological propositions about suicide, this content study dealt with suicide cases in the Kashmir province [in the state] which was unit of analysis. At the initial stage, news items reported in the local press were collected for a year. Subsequently, the data was aggregated and tabulated which provided the base for explanation/analysis of the suicides in the valley. At this stage, discussion was held with some experts. That enabled us to formulate the sociological propositions about the topic.

3. Findings of the Study

3.1. Number and Occumence of Suicides

The phenomenon of, suicide' was near-absent in the traditional Kashmiri society. But, at present, it has emerged as a significant social phenomenon.

Though this act on the part of individual has attained crucial importance in the valley, this phenomenon has not been studied seriously and academically by the social observers and other experts. Consequently, there is hardly any data, in terms of actual number or estimates, available on this topic.

There are two basic methods for getting the relevant data. These are the empirical investigation and [ii] study of reports about suicides published in the local press. We opted for the second method. But, this method has certain limitations. It is because all cases of suicide have not been reported in the press. According to an unofficial estimate, about 40.00 per cent cases of suicide have been reported in the local press. I feel that about 50.00 per cent suicides in Kashmir have been reported in the local press.

On the basis of content study of suicide reports in the local press during the period September 1999 to August 2000, we are in a position to say that about 15 suicides were committed in a month on an average. More or less, the same estimate [30 suicides in 2 months] was made by a local English daily in July 2000. The details about suicides are as follows:

Table 1. Number of Suicides in Kashmir, 1999-2000

S.No	*Period*		*No. of Suicides*
1.	September	1999	17
2.	October	1999	20
3.	November	1999	18
4.	December	1999	11
5.	January	2000	13
6.	February	2000	13
7.	March	2000	14
8.	April	2000	15
9.	May	2000	12
10.	June	2000	19
11.	July	2000	17
12.	August	2000	16
	Total [12 months]		185
	1 month		15.41 [average]

It follows that about 2000 persons have committed/attempted suicides in Kashmir during the last one decade starting from 1990. The content study also revealed that about 23.00 per cent persons were saved from death by their family members and in different health centers/hospitals.

As the local press reported, suicides were spread throughout the valley. The occurrence- pattern, especially rise and fall of suicides was determined by various factors. The occurrence-pattern of suicides covered in this study showed the up-down pattern revealing in Fig. 1 which follows:

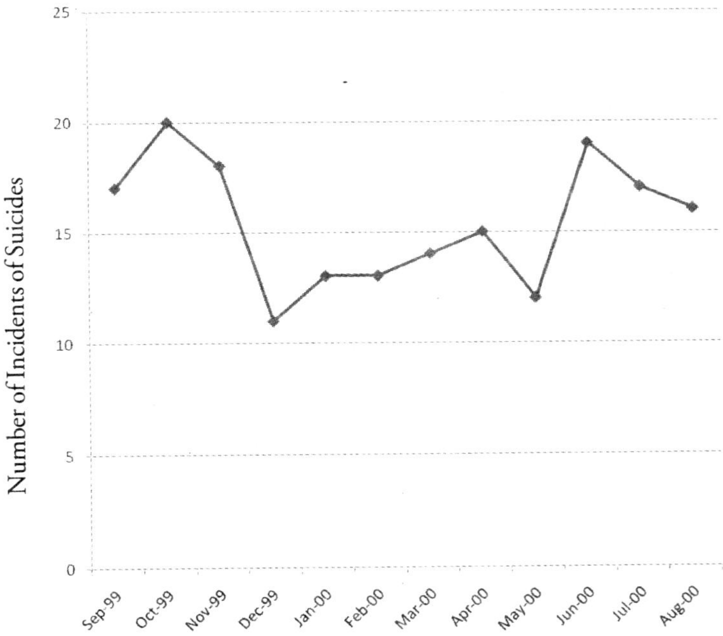

Fig 1. Suicides in the Kashmir Valley: 1999-2000.

Source: Local Newspapers, Srinagar, J&K.

It may not be out of place to mention here this content study is primarily sociological in nature. The major propositions developed in this report are fully supported by the relevant statistics. However, the arguments and figures are indicative, directional and revealing trends and patterns.

3.2. Male-Female Ratio-J&K

The cases of suicide reported in the local press were 77.4 I per cent females and 22.58 per cent males. It also revealed that about 70.00 per cent females were house-wives, while about 30.00 per cent females were working women This huge number/proportion of females in comparison to the males was attributed to their [women's] lesser patience, lesser care inside and outside families, lesser exposure to unprecedented violent situation, discrimination and harassment.

3.3. Rural-urban Ratio-J&K

The content-study divulged that among all reported cases of suicide, while 85.71 per cent Suicides were committed in rural areas, 14.28 per cent suicides were committed in urban areas. Primarily this extremely unequal proportion of suicides committed in rural and urban areas can be related to the demographic population of these two different areas, which according to 199l census was 74.00 per cent rural and 26.00 per cent urban. This may go against the conventional view upheld even by experts that the suicide rate is generally higher in urban areas than in rural areas. But, the different pattern of suicides in Kashmir can be explained in termof impact of armed conflict on population dynamics in general and on particular groups and sub-groups in particular.

3.4. Religious Affiliation-J&K

The content study showed that the dominant majority [i.e., 95.23 per cent of the total] of those who committed suicide in Kashmir were local Muslims belonging both major sects Sunnis and Shias. One other case of suicide of a Muslim was reported in the local press. He was a Bihari Iabourer working in the valley for many years All others who committed suicide and were reported were Hindus. Their proportion was about 4.00 per cent of the total suicides. All of them were outsiders and were working here for many years While some of them were working in armed forces, others were serving in central government offices.

3.5. Age-groups Ratio J&K

Our study reflected the participation of different age-groups in committing suicides as follows:

Table 2. Age-group Composition of Suicide-doers

S.No.	*Age Group*	*Participation in Suicides [per cent]*
01	06-15 years	03.07
02	16-25 years	76.92
03	26-40 years	20.00
04	41-years and above	00.00

The most active age group in committing suicide belongs to 16-25 years This group of youngsters belonging to all demographic, economic, educational, social-cultural, occupational and other groups. They also have affiliation with all communities and castes. The second active age group in committing suicides belongs to 26-40 years The members of this group are generally senior, mature and are settled in life comparatively. This group has more independence than the former group. The third group which has minor participation in suicides belongs to teenagers. They are very young and mostly students in colleges. Some of them became suicide-squads against the enemy.

3.6. Married-unmarried Ratio J&K

The content study showed that there was significant degree of difference between married and unmarried people who committed suicide. While the proportion of married was 40.32 per cent, the proportion of unmarried was 59.67 per cent. The higher proportion of unmarried in committing suicide [in comparison to married] can apparently be related to younger age-groups, lesser experience of very complex problems, and extensive as well as intensive impact of the militancy situation. Moreover, in the psychological framework, unmarried people have shown more tendency to suicide in comparison to their married counterparts.

3.7. Literate-illiterate Proportion J&K

The news report in local press gave no information about the literacy/ illiteracy status of the people who committed suicide in the valley in the last one year. In general, there is a feeling that more literate and less illiterate people have committed suicide in the recent past. Our inference conveys while about 60.00 per cent people [who committed suicide] were literate, about 40,00 per cent were illiterate. There is lso the feeling that literate people [who committed suicide] were more attached to social, economic, ideological and other related factors, while illiterate people were attached to marital, domestic and other related problems. It was also found that the literates attempt to suicide led to sure death but the attempt of the illiterates didn't prove sudden death.

3.8. Occupational Composition

The suicide reports in the local press did not mention the occupation of individuals who committed suicide. Since less information is available in this regard, there is very less clarity about the occupational composition of those who committed suicide However, our inference in this regard leads us to assume that most or the people who committed suicide in rural as well as urban areas were house-wives, even up to 65.00 per cent.The next significant group composed of the employees working in governmental and non- governmental office on lower/petty positions. The third group belonged to petty occupations and small business, especially in the urban areas.

3.9. Other Social Categories Ratio

In addition to the above mentioned groups and sub-groups of suicide-makers, other social categories composed of 27.41 per cent of the total.

[i] The first significant and distinctive group [in this series] composed of the students studying at pre-college and college level and their percentage was 72.17 per cent. They were very young [both boys and girls], belonging to the early and middle teens and showed desperation and frustration. Many of them committed suicide because they could not pass the examinations. Some of them were so committed ideologically and religiously that they find "suicide squads" and finished their lives for their cause. Some of them finished their lives simply because they had a dispute with their parents or other family membeRs

[ii] The second important group in the series composed of 'pregnant women' whose percentage was 11.96. Their compelling factors for taking extreme step of finishing their lives included marital disputes, economic compulsions, discrimination and harassment.

[iii] Another group, having the proportion of 5.88 per cent, composed of the personnel of the security forces/police. They belong to other parts of the country and have come here for their official work. It has been observed that living and service conditions are worse and they are not allowed even to proceed on leave. Moreover, they always live in fear. In this situation, they become frustrated and some of them ended their lives by committing suicide.

[iv] Still another group having 5.88 per cent proportion was of 'Bihari labourers' who have come here in recent years for work. This outside labour force, both skilled and unskilled, live in isolation but earn sufficient amount of money. Some of them have not been able to earn desired amount. Since they have come here with certain expectations which are not fulfilled in the prevailing conditions here so they prefer the escape way", i.e., the suicide.

[v] Another group which committed suicide was composed of the prisoners in the jails. Since the living conditions in the jails were worst and any protest meant dangerous consequences for the inmates" the jail prisoners preferred death through suicide.

3.10. Suicide Cases Registered by Police

Though the suicide rate in Kashmir is increasing fast, there has been no major, organised and continuous protest. The figures/percentage referred in this report are not more in comparison with the related situation prevailing in metro-politan areas, but even this number stands higher, even alarming, in the extremely traditional society of Kashmir. However, people about it at the individual and social level. In some cases this feeling reflected in their minor/peaceful protest followed by the registration of cases in police stations against persons considered responsible for compelling the persons to or creating the situation for committing suicide.

Among all cases of suicide about 31.00 per cent cases were registered in local police stations against the following categories of people:

In-laws of the suicide-maker	22.58 per cent
Husbands of the suicide-maker	12.90 per cent
Family members and relatives	09.67 per cent
Others-Unknown	54.81 per cent

It was found that though the above-mentioned cases were registered neither relatives [of suicide-makers] nor the police were serious in pursuing/following these cases till their logical end. Moreover, the police delay and relatives' apathy made the situation more tragic. The analysis of the reports of suicide cases revealed that the police took some action only in 13.62 per cent cases and that also under compulsion.

3.11. Methods of Commiting Suicide

The content study of news reports about suicide showed that it was committed by adopting the following methods:

[i]	Consuming poison	83.87 per cent
[ii]	Jumping in the river	06.45 per cent
[iii]	Self-immolation	04.83 per cent
[iv]	Hanging	03.22 per cent
[v]	Shooting with Gun	01.61 per cent

3.12. Apparent Reasons for Committing Suicide

The news in the local press about suicide in Kashmir reported the apparent reasons for committing suicide, which included the following [reasons]:

[i]	Extreme/heated arguments with parents/relative over general/particular and personal issues.	30.64 per cent
[ii]	Strained marital relations with husband/ disturbed marital life in the family/ wrong expectations about post-marital life	20.96 per cent
[iii]	Extreme poverty/very difficult economic conditions/unemployment	11.29 per cent
[iv]	Ill-treatment/discrimination/harassment of women by their in-laws	08.06 per cent
[v]	Father's/Guardian's death	06.45 per cent
[vi]	psychological depression/pathology	06.45 per cent
[vii]	Compulsion for marriage with the parental choice.	06.45 per cent
[viii]	To avoid rape by the security forces/other armed groups.	04.83 per cent
[ix]	Social factors	03. 22 per cent
[x]	Harassment/eve-teasing of young girls outside their homes.	01.61 per cent

3.13. Suicide Among Armed Forces

Like the phenomenon of suicide among the locals [civilians], it also exists among all sections of the armed forces, who all are outsiders and have been transferred here for a specific period. Though no exact figures about suicides among the security forces are available, the local press has reported several cases of suicide among them in last few years During the period of this study, more than two cases of suicide were reported, one belonging to the officer cadre and other to the lower cadre. The reasons for their suicide cited in the press included perpetual fear of death, alienation, worst life conditions, no social-cultural life and refusal of leave. All suicides in the armed forces were committed by shooting themselves. In some cases, the individual armed person killed himself and his colleagues or officeRs

3.14. Suicide Bombers

A new phenomenon emerged in the area of suicides in Kashmir in the context of armed conflict here in the last one decade. It was the emergence of "suicide bombers" which refers to the local youths, belonging to the teen age group, who killed themselves by striking with the Indian security installations, campus and other related places.

3.15. Concluding Points

The preceding details of the cases of suicides prove that a high rate of suicide has been experienced in the Kashmir valley in the previous one decade. So, it has emerged as very significant phenomenon here qualitatively as well as quantitatively. It may be necessary to mention here that there is no information, especially in terms of statistics, available about suicides in Kashmir in the past. Same is the case about suicides at present. In this situation, it is impossible to have a comparison between the past and present. Only inferences and estimates can help in this regard.

In the above-mentioned situation, it seems really difficult to talk about proper/particular reasons of suicides in Kashmir. However, on the basis of Scanty information which we got from the local newspapers, we may argue about the co-relation between the acts of suicide and various socio-economic and other factoRs It follows that the incidence of suicides in the valley may be explained in terms of varying degrees of social, psychological, educational, political, economic and other relevant factors. These acts may also be explained partly in terms of implication of the on-going militancy in the valley. Thus, the militancy has added certain other features to the acts of suicide in Kashmir such as their [suicides'] peculiarities which include sudden and fast increase in the number of acts of suicide; more number of suicides committed by females than males; more acts of suicide committed in rural areas than in urban areas; no mass, organised and continuous protest against the increasing suicides here; extreme ups and downs in the trends of suicides here; and no official, formal and complete record of suicides.

Though it is absolutely desirable and functionally necessary that the incidence of suicide in Kashmir must be totally stopped and finally eliminated. But, the total elimination of this phenomenon in the valley seems difficult, even not possible. In actuality, this process seems irreversible in the social dynamics of our society. However, it may be controlled to the maximum extent by the prevailing active social forces/ factors. In order to make this control more realistic and effective, serious and long-term efforts have to be carried out at the psychological, family and broader social levels. In this regard, reference may be made to the social environment created during the month of *RAMADAN*, which recorded the least number of suicides [11 in a month] during the previous year as well as this year.

Last, but not the least, it may be noted that there emerges an urgent and basic need to record all cases of suicides formally by the governmental and non-governmental organisations/ agencies and make detailed studies of suicides by the professionals, academicians and other experts. This will certainly help in the formulation and implementation of relevant policy/ programmes to control and eliminate suicides in Kashmir.

4. Other Features of Suicides in Kashmir

The present study on suicides in Kashmir for the period 04/2009 - 06/ 2011, other sociological features were reflected in the press reports. Some of these distinctive features are explained below:

[i] *Higher/highest number and rate of suicide:* While the total number of suicides committed during 2009-2011 was 227 as per the reports published in the local daily newspapeRs This number represented the part of the total number of suicides committed and recorded formally in health/medical centres and police stations in all areas. However, the number of suicides published in the local print media reveals categorically the higher/highest number and rate of suicides and their direction is further increased.

[ii] *Women and Suicides:* It was reported repeatedly in the local press that females outnumber males in committing suicides in rural and urban

areas in Kashmir. In fact, the press proved more conscious and alert in reporting the suicide incidents of females. It was generally assumed in the local media that suicide rate among females was higher than among males. It was consistently upheld that major causes of more suicides were related to family disorganisation, domestic problems, gender disputes, matrimonial matters, harassment by in-laws, dowry demand, and different kinds of discrimination. In actuality, the perpetual armed conflict and its non-stop implications effected adversely the family and its environment in such a way that hurt the female absolutely, especially after their marriage. So, they suffered in every field of life. It was in the context of these conflict and non-conflict determined factors which compelled necessarily the female of all age groups to opt for ending life miserably through committing suicides.

[iii] *Youth, Students and Suicides*

[a] The local print media in Kashmir published regular reports about suicides among the youth, especially the students. Many newspapers published editorials repeatedly, in addition to daily news items on front/middle pages, about increasing trend of suicides among the youth. [see Srinagar Times, Srinagar, 4th June 2009 and 18th May 2010]. It was generally reported the youth composed of the most dominant and most active group among those who committed suicide in Kashmir and ended their lives voluntarily. A particular daily newspaper [Srinagar Times, Srinagar, 18th May 2010] quoted a particular age group of 15 - 30 years which stands the most active group of suicide-makeRs Other newspapers also cited more or less same age group for committing more suicides comparatively.

[b] The local media characterised this large number of suicides by youth as unprecedented. It put forward the idea that this type of situation never prevailed in the entire recorded history of Kashmir. The local media opined on the causation and implications of large number of 'youth suicides'. Every newspaper wrote several editorials and published many papers, articles and news-analysis on this topic. In general, the local media argued that this situation occurred in Kashmir mainly due to the environment of conflict in continuity for two long decades. That environment was characterised by highest degree of tension, depression, stress, anxiety, fear, threat, insecurity, etc. Moreover, the youth in Kashmir became the major target of

security forces in this highly volatile environment. The longevity of the conflict situation added fuel to the fire and frustrated, brutalised and dehumanised the entire youth. In that situation, the youth felt that there was no alternative in life except to commit suicide. In this way, the act of suicide got wider social legitimacy and many youth ended their lives. Finally, the local print media argued that a full generation got lost and they lost everything from career to worldview and so need a radical change in order to save them.

[c] Among the youth, the dominant group composed of students, especially of medium and higher stages for one apparent reason or the other. According to a leading local daily newspaper [Srinagar Times, Srinagar, 4th June 2009], one out of every five suicides belong to the student community. They composed 33 - 36 per cent of the total number of youth who committed suicide. [*Ibid.* They belonged to school, college and university level institutions. The local media revealed that more literates than illiterates were involved in suicide-making. Thus a huge number of students lost their lives and their families had to face the pathetic impact. Most of the suicides among students occurred at the time of examination results. When students could not concentrate on studies due to widespread pathology, tension, depression, insecurity and physical threat, they perform miserably in the exams. And so become 'failures'. At that time, they get psychologically frustrated and dejected and thrown-out beings, so they feel about one escape route only, i.e., suicide. When the number of failures remained constant or increased, the number of suicides too remained constant or increased heavily.

[d] According to the local press reports, the other major factor which compelled students to commit suicides was their continuous harassment and torture inside as well as outside educational institutions on the part of security forces and local police. In fact, they remained one of the major targets of security agencies and forces in Kashmir, especially in the counter-insurgency operations. The added disadvantages were poverty, unemployment and corruption. With these major-minor sociological factors, which can directly be related to the long-term implications of the armed conflict in Kashmir, the local press analysed the problems faced by the students in the present-day conditions.

5. Religion and Suicide

[i] An interesting topic touched by the local media in reporting suicide cases was the role of religion in the acts of committing suicides in Kashmir. These newspapers wrote many editorials, published many stories, articles and columns, and made several news-analysis about orientation and role of the dominant religion in Kashmir, i.e., Islam, and the behaviour of its followers, i.e., Muslims. It was clearly reported in all newspapers that in no way it has allowed committing suicide in any situation. In fact, Islam has completely forbidden it and considers it a 'sin'. Thus it, in clear cut and absolute terms dubbed it as against religion and legally stopped its manifestations, tendencies and encouragement. The Islamic perception about life, as portrayed by the local media in English as well as Urdu languages, was presented as positive, purposeful and socially-naturally suitable. According to this perception, human life is considered as the kindest and most valuable gift of God, which must neither be wasted nor finished purposelessly. It must be lived with proper identity, supreme dignity and live in consonance with laws-rules of the nature given by God in religious scriptures to all people of the world at different times and in different languages.

[ii] The local press also upheld the view that there must not be provided any justification even for the idea of suicide. The ideal position of Islam, mentioned above, was emphasised repeatedly by all newspapeRs This media also upheld the view that all qualified and concerned scholars, Ulema, theologians and intellectuals have unanimously agreed that there can be no justification for committing suicides as Islam has categorically banned it. In fact, they considered it completely irreligious and totally un-Islamic. The media also presented the view that all authentic sources of Islam, especially Quran and Haidth, oppose or negate clearly and completely the act of suicide and characterise it as 'irreligious' and 'anti'religious'.

[iii] In other words, the local media conveyed the message that every religion abhors suicide, so, it must be considered undesirable and must be necessarily condemned. The individual must not even think of committing these irreligious acts. On the one hand, the local media conveyed that suicide stands as the religious and legal offence. So, it must be avoided at all costs. On the other hand, it stressed on individuals, organisations and groups to resist it positively and strongly. It also called upon all social classes and communities to exert and resist actively the act of suicide.

Finally, it appealed to the government and civil society to play a positive and active role in stopping the crime of suicide in Kashmir.

[iv] But, at the same time, the local press revealed the existing reality of everyday life in Kashmir. It was that despite the absolute religious opposition, suicides continue in Kashmir unabated. In fact, the reports reveal that the number and rate of suicides has increased continuously over last many years [The 'suicide diary' in this book established this point reasonably.] The religious condemnation of suicides seems to have no significant impact on the increasing trend of committing suicides. Thus this phenomenon expands and intensifies day by day in Kashmir. In actuality, it was found in the local press that in one case, a religious preacher [included in the 'suicide diary'] himself committed suicide. In the second case [also included in 'suicide diary'], a young boy committed suicide by hanging from the fan just after he finished his evening prayers. In other cases too, it was found that extremely religious persons committed suicide on one apparent reason or the other. Thus the religious attitudes and behaviour too could not change the direction of the tide of suicides in Kashmir.

6. The Reformative Campaign

[i] Out of the context of irreligiosity of suicide, a strong trend of campaign against this act was born in Kashmir through the local media. Accordingly, while several editorials, columns, articles and news-analysis were published repeatedly to negate the concept and practice of suicides in Kashmir, many practical measures were suggested for the government and civil society for total elimination of this social problem. The local print media called upon the religious scholars and preachers to emphasise the irreligious character of suicide to distract the youth from these tendencies. It also stressed the role of intellectuals and scholars in this systematic and organised campaign. Finally, it also called on the government to solve core and crucial problems of seven youth, such as unemployment, poverty and corruption, so that they don't feel compelled to resort to this drastic and dreadful act.

[ii] But, as the fact stands, suicides in Kashmir have not stopped despite this continuous and sustained campaign against it. In reality, these have increased in numbers and rates despite reformative campaign. It may be argued that there are certain set factors, such as economic, psychological and political factors, which determine the nature and trends of suicide.

These factors can not be ignored in the explanation of suicides. It follows that the act of suicide is a religious act primarily, so it cannot be resolved totally by the religious persuation. Since it stands as the 'social act', it may be resolved through social efforts only. This approach towards suicides in Kashmir may prove more relevant, more useful and more productive.

1. The Suicide Note

[i] A 'suicide note' of a person who commits a suicide or makes an attempted suicide represents the real [and truthful] statements, emotions and compulsions. It also throws light on the complex factors or necessary causation about the 'successful act' of suicide. It become the base for post-suicide investigation and explanation of the deadly act. The local print media quoted partly or fully published from these 'suicide notes'. A local weekly newspaper published the full text of a 'suicide note' of a person who attempted suicide but failed. [swell] This note throws light on various sociological aspects of this act of suicide. Sine this reveals comprehensively the social character of suicide, we present it here in original:

"...It is limelight winter evening , I stand firm on my decision, while searching the deepest point in the Jhelum. I am not one of those water environmentalists nor a typical nature lover. I disown the paradox, world and this city. It has amplified my every effort into a debacle.

I am fed up with this rat race and non-negotiable give ups: In fact I may get at least some relaxation before being burnt in hell for eternity, as the common belief is. So, here am I, wishing good bye to the world of pain and only pain; Saying 'that is it' No more now.' By now your guess work is perfect; I am aspirant of suicide. Since afternoon I have been walking the streets of Lal Chowk waiting for the crowds to disperse, so that no one turns up to ... save me! That's right!

Though today it appears like no one has a home or, like watchmen they will spend the night on the roads. While waiting, I have wasted enough energy to force myself to rest. Sitting alongside beggars on the bridge completely recognising the irony - they are here begging for life and ... I". For a fraction of a minute I think good of life, then shake the thoughts out of my mind pondering at my own disastrous experiences. Eventually my eyes get heavier and my body becomes a little tipsy.

In no time ... a man is standing on the bridge looking towards the sky, muttering something to himself. A tear rolls down his face plummeting in to the muddy water. Steadily, he widens the distance between his arms, his heart pumps blood like a gush as he anticipates the outcome. Meanwhile he closes his eyes ... and jumps!

My senses are choked from conveying anything. Somehow I titter to see him fall. Briefly I notice other faces in the same posture observing the same thing time and again till it all is a trite site. After that there is a lull but not before I witness trepidation. Some mob comes out from nowhere reaching the bridge and they act in congruence with the previous men. Again there is this killing silence followed by another kill. This cycle goes on, and on, till a conundrum of quietness comes into existence, an unpleasant calm overshadows everything! Now of course, it is no more a boring activity but full of apprehension and anxiety. It seems the city is nearly empty; none, nowhere.

I break into sweat - from my red, hot forehead, almost turning unconscious with fear. I think endlessly of what I am going to do? No people!!!! No one! Completely frightened by the notion of total solitariness. The vacuous spaces and streets turn me into a statue, into a man who is suddenly transported to another world.

"This is the real hell, is it hell?" Hence I perform an involuntary action, in future to do, only the purpose is an absolute contrast. Repeating the same old trick of stretching arms, a tear. Closed eyes and not to forget, the jump!

As I am nearing the water, I become conscious of some known sounds, first from the near-by temple, then the invitation from the mosque, the muezzin crying, "Come towards God, come towards success". The moment I strike the water my hands start hurting me. My eye instantly opens up, I am on the bridge! On the footpath! Initially I felt I am dead. But seeing people coming out of their houses, with certainty I sum up, that for the whole night, I had been sleeping here. The most important part of it was only a nightmare! I walk to the edge of the bridge, observe the river punctiliously and smile!

As the sun rises, I journey back home. May be there are some interesting things stored in life."[6]

In response to this and other suicide notes [and attempts of committing suicide at large], there was a response from a reader of a local newspaper who wrote an open letter to all those who intend to commit suicide.[7] This letter was extremely emotional [but rational too] and religious in content. The reader made an argument that since the religion of Islam has prohibited suicide, there seems no ground or justification for committing this sinful act. Moreover, he continued, the suicide ruins the other world also as God is not happy with this act. In this context, he appealed to all members of society, particularly the youth, to avoid killing themselves in all situations and live an honourable, religious, dignified and civilised life.

2. Potential Cases of Suicide in Kashmir

[i] In the preceding sections of this chapter, we explained/analysed various sociological features of acts of suicide in Kashmir during last three years as reported in the local print media. In this section, we have identified many potential cases of suicide in Kashmir, whether successful or not, which were highlighted specifically by the local newspapers and gave sociological bits of information about these acts before or after this incident took place. In other words, the news items/stories convey details about social causation, social dynamics, social background and social implications which we intend to highlight here. In addition, it is the social relevance and particular context which provided the criteria for selecting these news items/reports/stories/analysis in this chapter. Here we present these news items, etc.

[a] An attendant of a patient admitted in SKIMS, Soura, Srinagar committed suicide by jumping from the window on Friday night. He was attending his father in ward no. 6 A jumped out at 1.30 a.m. He had a verbal duel with his father before committing suicide. Police has registered a case under FIR.[8]

[b] A girl, 23, tried to end her life after she found that her pre-paid mobile phone was not working while trying to reach out to her friend. A resident of Chattergul in Ganderbal district, she had consumed some poisonous substance after she failed to connect with her friend on Sunday. However, she was discharged from the hospital on Monday after a stomach wash[9]

[c] A young man hanged himself on a tree in Shopian district which sent a shockwave in the entire town. The concerned person, after evening prayers, went directly to his room for sleeping. When the family tried to wake him up in the morning, there was no response from inside. When the door was opened forcibly, they were shocked to see his body hanging from the room fan.[10]

[d] A newly-wed groom who had married only a month back was found hanged on the tree.... In Kulgam district, 17 day old bride committed suicide and ended her life by consuming poison, the common method

used for committing suicides in Kashmir.... In Anantnag district too, a young girl consumed poison and ended her life.[11]

[e] Not bearing the burden of this world, three women preferred consuming poison and ending their lives. The first consumed the gel poison and the second used the pesticides meant for horticulture purpose. The third hanged herself.[12]

[f] A student of 12th class committed suicide in Ganderbal district. People were shocked over this incident and they made a mass protest against government authorities and stoned all passing vehicles. He consumed poisonous substance in uncle's home. He was taken to the hospital where he could not be saved. No apparent reason/s has been quoted in this case. Police has started investigation officially.[13]

[g] Shad left Kashmir in 2007 and Z in 2008. One had gone to Bangalore and the second to Delhi. When they met a week back in Kashmir on the banks of Dal, their thought went to two people, who were no longer in this world. S's thoughts went to his brother - M. and Z's went to his girl friend, A. Both had committed suicide. "I see him in my dreams," says S. M was just 16 year old when he killed himself. "I sometimes still question myself why this happened ? Why did I slap him that day? Says S with tears in his eyes. M had not been a good student and was not interested in studies. He preferred to spend most of his time at his father's pharmaceutical shop. This worried his parents. " I wanted to become an engineer, and my brother wanted to become a salesman," says S., who is in the final year of his engineering course. On the day M. committed suicide, everything had seemed normal to the family. The family had to attend a get-together at a close relative's house who had returned from Hajj. Earlier M. had failed in the exam. And he found little sense in continuing.[14]

[h] A. on the contrary, had been brought up in a very understanding environment. She went to one of the best schools in the valley, had all the facilities, everything she desired. A. met Z. first at tuition class during class 11. The two started helping each other with studies and soon developed a good friendship. They fell in love. "She was very mild and she would even get angry at me." He says. Z. is still at a loss to understand what happened. We met on the morning of that day and everything was okay. After the school, Z. waited for her at the spot where they used to meet every day. But, she did not come. Z. kept calling her phone, but it

was switched off. He thought that she would turn up at tutors'. But, she did not. Z. never saw her again.[15]

[i] R.S., 30, from Anantnag district is undergoing treatment in the hospital. He had attempted suicide by consuming pesticides. He was saved as his family took him to a hospital in time. He says he tried to commit suicide because of economic reasons. He is the only brother of four sisters and much is expected of him. His family is in shock but he is recovering.[16]

[j] B.A. too attempted suicide. He tried to cut his veins, but the timely intervention of his family saved him. He was unemployed for a long time. "For every case of suicide, there are around 8 cases of such attempted suicides", says his doctor.[17]

[k] R.B., a 20 year old girl from Bhaleesa [Jammu region] was pursuing her education in Kishtwar district. She was on her way to Ramban to meet her classmate who was also on his way to Kishtwar. Their buses stopped at pul-Doda for tea on a roadside stall. They were interrupted and the local SPO humiliated and beat Dar and threatened the girl for relationship with Dar. They were taken to the police station where from girl's father was conveyed her alleged relationship with Dar. She ran away from the police station and jumped in to the nearby river wherefrom she could not be recovered.[18]

[l] On March17, 2009, S.B. who was in her 20s set herself afire and was admitted in to a local hospital with 90 per cent burns. She died a day later. Resident of Kathua district [Jammu region] she in her dying statement accused the SPOs of exploiting her continuously. They were rounded up and investigation has started.[19]

References

1. See M. Phil. Dissertation of Aijaz Ahmad Mir entitled Trends of Crime in the Kashmir Valley: A Sociological Study in Srinagar District, submitted in the Department of Sociology, University of Kashmir, Srinagar. The research was carried out under the supervision of the author January 2012.
2. *Ibid.*
3. See local print media reports, analysis, articles, columns and editorials in this regard.
4. *Ibid.*
5. *Ibid.*

6. Kashmir Life, Srinagar, May 2010.
7. Srinagar Times, Srinagar, 3.7.2010.
8. *Ibid.*, 4.10.2010.
9. *Ibid.*, 3.4.2011
10. *Ibid.*, 31.9.2010.
11. *Ibid.*, 31.10.2010.
12. *Ibid.*, 23.9.2010.
13. *Ibid.*, 5.8.2010.
14. Kashmir Life, Srinagar, 19.06.2011
15. *Ibid.*
16. *Ibid.*
17. *Ibid.*
18. *Ibid.*
19. *Ibid.*, 11.12.2011.

15

Unprcedented Rise of Violence Against Women in Kashmir

1. **Introduction — Domestic Violence Against Women [DVAW]**

1.1. In general, DVAW refers to a social phenomenon which reveals violent as well as non-violent behaviour of male members of society towards female members of society in and around domestic framework, especially after the marital life of women start. It includes all types of attitudes and behaviours related to the personal and social interests of women in post-marital life. It involves all verbal and physical acts which abuse, hurt and violate against women in general on the part of men related through marriage. In actuality, this phenomenon stands not only as the inter-sex phenomenon but as the intra-sex phenomenon too in the broader social dynamics. In operational sense, DVAW represent "the force whether overt or covert used to wrest from an individual [a woman] something she does not want to give of her own free will and which causes her either physical injury or emotional trauma or both."

1.2. In Sociology, the topic off violence against women [VAW] is treated in broader network. In the sociological disciplinary framework, the following typology of VAW has been developed mainly on the basis of major themes and characteristics of each type:

[i] Criminal violence against women;

[ii] Domestic violence against women; and

[iii] Social violence against women.

The first type of VAW is criminal violence which reflects in the violent acts of rape, murder, abduction and bride-burning and invites strongest punishment including hanging and sentenced to death on the part of courts. While this crime is committed by men against women in general but women's support and help in it can not be ruled out in all cases. It happens within and outside the domestic limits/boundaries. The second type of VAW is known as domestic violence against women' which usually takes place within the limits of domestic field that generally starts after marriage of women. This type of violence reflects in wife-beating, mental and physical torture, sexual abuse and maltreatment of widows within the home environment, molestation, robbing of earned money and so on. This violence specifically takes place within the family boundaries after the married life starts at the residence of in-laws. In many cases, it is initiated and perpetrated with direct provocation of female members of that family, especially mothers-sisters-in-law. This inside violence stands as one-sided violence and is always directed against women and their interests. The third type of VAW has been called as 'social violence' which generally occurs inside as well as outside homes and involve generally all non-violent acts. The acts include mental torture, haraassment, eve-teasing, female foeticide, denial of several rights, force for committing sati, snatching the earnings of the working daughters in law and many other acts against women on the part of men. [See Ram Ahuja, Social Problems in India, New Delhi, 1997, Rawat Publications]

1.3. The sociological characterisation of these types of VAW can be explained in terms of their direct, necessary and reciprocal relationship. We may formulate an argument that VAW cannot be compartmentalised and studied in parts or in isolation. Thus it seems clear that VAW in private sphere is directly and necessarily related to VAW in public sphere and vice versa. These propositions are more applicable in the context of Kashmir. However, the scope of this paper is narrow and limited to the theme of DVAW in Kashmir [DVAWK] which will be analysed in all its features and manifestations in this paper.

2. DVAWK

2.1. It is believed that traditional Kashmiri society about 100 years back was considered a completely non-violent society. The attitude and behaviour of people were oriented towards peace, harmony and concensus, while social ethos was totally non-violent. It has been observed/reported that people at large were neither involved in nor heard about minor or major violent act. This social situation provides the rationale for the characterisation of Kashmiris as non-violent people. In this context, though women represented a dominated, subjugated and maltreated lot, violence and crime was not used against them in an organised and systematic way.

2.2. However, the situation has changed radically due to various developments in the last century and particularly in last two decades. The century-spread developments include processes of change and development, especially modernisation, urbanisation, industrialisation, migration, materialistic outlook which transformed entire life-style in Kashmir qualitatively as well as quantitatively. In social dynamics related to these developments, women at large were exposed to the positives and negatives of modern life . In this way, the Kashmiri society joined the mainstream of developing societies which also gave rise to varied crucial problems for women. Subsequently, in the recent decades, the social environment created by the forces of militancy and militarisation increased and intensified this phenomenon of VAWK, especially of criminal nature. This new trend has exposed entire womenfolk to extreme forms of violence and cruelty within and outside the domestic framework. In reality, this inhuman trend has crossed all civilised limits and consequently hundreds and thousands of local women have been raped, murdered, molested, tortured, harassed, abused, offended, dishonoured and maltreated.

2.3. DVAW in the Kashmiri society was introduced in modern times in a systematic and institutionalised way through two major gateway situations. The first major series of social processes was related to broader social transformation due to changs in this background, with attainment of modern education and adoption of regular-remunerative employment by women in large numbers gave rise to dual role of women [one at home and other in office] created a situation of role conflict for them. This gave rise to many serious problems for them at both places. In actuality, while women faced one set of problems in traditional situation such as dependency, denial of rights and discrimination, they now encountered a new set of problems such as post-marital discard, harassement and torture.

2.4. The second series of social processes was related to the entry of women in post-marital life situation. Though women were becoming increasingly educated and economically independent, the societal attitude and behaviour towards this new role of women could not be changed in equal proportion. Thus a situation of change and continuity emerged in this context. It can be explained in a way that though women's economic independence through self-earning/employment was achieved, it could not be availed fully due to snatching of this money by in-laws family in considerable number of cases. In this changing situation, the post-marital life brought numerous problems for significant number of women which include mental-physical torture, harassment, post-marital disharmony/ discard, dowry demand and bride-burning. This behaviour against women also included many violent acts of wife-beating, physical torture and dowry deaths. In this situation, even clear religious injunctions and moral codes were violated. Islamic orders regarding separation, divorce, maintenance, inheritance rights, full and timely payment of mahr and so on were not followed seriously and completely. It was essentially in this social context that a law about domestic violence against women was implemented in 2008.

3. **Study of Dvawk in Kashmir [DVAWK study, 194]**

3.1. *Methodology:* A sociological study about DVAWK was carried out in 2002-03. The universe of this study is the Kashmir province which composed of all six administrative districts of Srinagar, Anantnaag, Baramulla, Budgam, Pulwama and Kupwara. The sample of the study composed of 200 women respondents selected on the basis of sociological criteria/variables of age, literacy, income, rural-urban and marital status, family structure and working status. The necessary data-information was collected by trained research investigators through questionnaire and interview techniques. The participant observation method was also used. After collecting required data-information, it was aggregated, tabulated and explained rationally.

3.2. *Some Major Findings*

3.2.1. *Discrimination against women:* The first important finding was that systematic discrimination against women is going on in the social life in Kashmir. It reveals in the following table:

Table 1. Discrimination against women within families

S.No.	*Response*	*S.*	*Ba.*	*Bm.*	*A.*	*P.*	*K.*	*Total*
1.	Yes	68.00	60.00	60.00	63.33	66.66	56.66	63.00
2.	No	32.00	40.00	40.00	36.33	33.33	43.33	37.00

While majority of respondents, 63.00 per cent feel that the practice of discrimination against women in family existed at large, minority of them, 37.00 per cent, felt otherwise. Though these responses can be explained in relation to different variables, in general it was observed that women get discriminated usually. But, it was also observed that dominant trend of change is expanding fast. The areas in which the above-mentioned women were discriminated were as follows:

[i] education 16.00 per cent
[ii] gifts 23.00 per cent
[iii] clothes 11.00 per cent
[iv] diet/food 24.00 per cent
[v] ownership 13.00 per cent
[vi] decision-making 35.00 per cent
[vii] property 54.00 per cent
[viii] social treatment 30.00 per cent
[ix] employment 18.00 per cent

3.2.2. *Women working role:* In the post-marital life, women get different kinds of treatment from in-laws families which may be characterised as positive [i.e., appreciative] or negative [i.e., condemnatory]. In this regard, the respondents in this study gave the response noted in the following table:

Table 2. Treatment of in-laws families towards working women's role

S.No.	*Response*	*S.*	*B*	*B*	*A.*	*P.*	*K.*	*Total*
1.	Appreciation	26.47	14.70	14.70	17.64	14.70	11.76	39.08
2.	Condemnation	25.92	14.81	18.51	14.81	11.11	14.81	31.03
3.	Both	23.07	19.23	15.38	19.23	11.53	11.53	29.88

The table reveals that 39.08 per cent women got appreciation, while 31.03 per cent women got condemnation. At the same time, 29.88 per cent women got both kinds of responses on the part of their respective in-laws families. It follows that a significant number of women didn't get appreciation from in-laws family which spoiled the normal post-marital life of concerned women. This undesirable response reflected in jeleosy, teasing, harassment, mental and physical torture, discrimination, snatching of money, dowry demand and so on.

3.2.3. *Separation between the couple:* The continuous post-marital strain and discard often leads to separation between husband and wife, which continues for years and decades. In our study, we got the following number of husband-wife separation cases:

Srinagar district	5
Baramulla district	5
Budgam district	6
Anantnag district	5
Pulwama district	3
Kupwara district	4
Total	28

The particular reasons for separation were given by the concerned women as follows:

Undesirable behaviour/torture by in-laws family members	7
Misunderstanding between husband and wife	4
Husband's suspicion about his wife's extra marital relations	5
Govt. job of women and its impact on family	1
Love affair of the husband with other girl	1
Physical assault on wife causing physical damage	2
Initiative for establishing separate nuclear family unit	2
Husband was forced to marry the present wife	2
Economic problems	2
Husband's ill treatment	2
Total	28

In most of such cases, women [and children, if any] are the real suffers because they don't get any maintenance. It was also found that while husbands were interested in compromise in many cases, the family member prolonged the period of separation by their intervention and making more demands. Very less number of such women, i.e., 14 per cent, approached courts for justice, while 64 per cent and 14 per cent approached near-relatives and social notables respectively for any solution.

3.2.4. *Practice of wife-beating*: This study revealed that a significant number of women get regular beating by their husbands. It is clear from the following table:

Table 3. Practice of wife-beating by their husbands

S.No.	*Response*	*S.*	*B*	*B*	*A.*	*P.*	*K.*	*Total*
1.	Yes	22.00	18.00	15.00	16.00	14.00	14.00	31.84
2.	No	19.62	17.75	13.69	14.95	14.95	14.01	68.15

The table shows that 32 per cent of women get regular beating by their husbands after their marriage, more in rural than in urban areas, while 68 per cent women were not experiencing this inhuman practice. It was also observed that in some cases not only husbands but other family members too involve themselves in this practice. Regarding the reccurance of this practice, it was found that 18 per cent respondents were beaten twice, thrice or four times, while 7 per cent were beaten more than three times. 75 per cent respondents revealed their beating once in life time. The apparent causes for wife-beating were identified as follows:

Efforts to establish new nuclear family 20.00 per cent

Suspicion of husband about his wife's extra marital relations 20.00 per cent

Bad food preparation 5.00 per cent

Talking with neighbours about marital disharmony 5.00 per cent

Husband wanted to marry another girl 10.00 per cent

Improper handling of household things 10.00 per cent

Exchange of heated arguments with husbands 10.00 per cent

Husbands were short tempered 10.00 per cent

Husbands feeling of superiority and domination 10.00 per cent

It was also observed that there was no active resistance to this brutal practice on the part of women. Conversely, a smaller number of women tried to put justification for it.

3.2.5. *Torture and harassment:* This study found that 40 per cent of respondents faced torture and harassment in their post-marital life on the part of in-laws family members, both men and women. These practices were organised and systematic and their examples were as follows:

Creating conditions for mental disturbance;

Hurting and abusing and offending without any reason;

Providing basis of tension and anxiety within families;

Physical beating;

Showing no satisfaction on the work performed by daughter-in-law;

Never treating us equal and well;

Unnecessary interference in our personal affairs;

Getting all household works done by us; showing arrogance, superiority and domination on us;

Asking us to give personal things to them;

Grabbing of the amount of salary;

Attempts to humiliate us on important occasions;

Imposing forcefully all decisions on us;

Always finding faults in our work and behaviour; and

Giving us the feeling that we are worth nothing.

It was observed that 14 per cent women approached their parents and relatives regarding this matter while 28 per cent tolerated all this silently. Only 14 per cent respondents reacted sharply and showed strong, open and continuous opposition. According to respondents, the ways and methods through which these practiced could be stopped were as mentioned below:

Mass education to all	32.00 per cent
Separation from parental household and stablishment of nuclear family	34.00 per cent
Developing mutual understanding between husband & wife	9.00 per cent
Overall social transformation	4.00 per cent
To raise consciousness among women about their rights	11.00 per cent
It is very difficult to stop these practices	10.00 per cent

3.2.6. *Demand of dowry:* Usually, problems for women in post-marital life start with the demand of dowry by in-laws family. While in some cases, this demand is met, in other cases it is not met leading to cruel acts against daughters-in-law. In our study, 9 per cent women were demanded dowry by the in-laws who included husband and others. It also divulged that 25 per cent respondents gave various items to in-laws family, while 75 per cent refused. These items included colour television, maruti car, furniture items, locker, bed, carpets, land, cash certificates, gold jewellery, refrigerator, washing machine, costly clothes, watch, VCR-VCP and costly gifts.

3.2.7. *Threat to divorce:* This study revealed that 23 per cent of respondents were given the threat to divorce. But, at the same time, while 5 per cent men practiced it, 95 per cent didn't practice it. It follows that though this problem exists in Kashmir but its intensity is not deep and its occurance is not frequent. Kashmiris in general consider divorce as "highly undesirable".

3.2.8. *Molestation:* The findings of this study were that while 33 per cent respondents faced/observed/heard/read about cases of molestation of women, 42 per cent didn't face/observe/heard/read about such cases within and outside domestic framework. The acts of molestation were performed by near relatives [9/30], distant relatives [7/30], neighbours [14/30], office colleagues [10/26], young unknown persons [2/26], and armed forces [10/26] These acts of molestation were committed at residential houses [26/66], public places/roads [12/66], offices/places of work [10/66], agricultural fields [9/66], and public parks [9/66]. The apparent reasons for committing molestation were reported as raids by the armed forces [16/66], over-crowd in public buses [11/66], love related matters [8/66], enemity/jealousy of working women [6/66], sexual lust [7/66], indecent dress of women [4/66], physical beauty of women [2/66], acts of Juvenile delinquency [6/66], and impact of hindi films [6/66].

3.2.9. *Role of female sex:* This study divulged the fact that it is not men only but women too impose cruelty against women in the domestic framework. The respondents conveyed the following views in this regard:

Women tortured us more	[32.00 per cent]
Women played a vital/major role in violence against us	[55.00 per cent]
The violent behaviour in in-laws families was based on the wishes of all women	[20.00 per cent]
Women were initiators & perpetrators of domestic violence against us	[44.00 per cent]

16

Emergence of Late Marriage in Kashmir

1. Introduction

It has been established with a lot of sociological evidence that every human society has decided about marriage at a particular age. It has also been observed that various factors such as cultural, religious, psychological, educational, political, societal, economic, demographic and other contributed to this phenomenon. Thus, at present, we face a situation at the global level in which some societies, especially modernised societies, have developed comparatively higher age of marriage, while other societies, especially modernising societies, have maintained comparatively lower age of marriage. In this theoretical background, the phenomenon of early and late marriage needs to be seen in multi-dimensional context and sociological perspective.

Sociologically, late marriage refers to a situation in which marriages are generally solemnised much after the normal or average or desirable age of marriage. It varies from late teens to late twenties for males as well as females. This situation generally arises in the context of limitless impact of the processes of modernisation. However, in certain situations, a particular factor such as political or economic emerges as the dominant and determining factor for changing the nature, criteria and consequences of late marriage.

The above-mentioned sociological propositions about late marriage can be applied to the existing situation in the Kashmiri society. The impact of multi-farious developments during last 60 years related to the practice of late marriage can be explained in two specific points. First, socio-economic and educational-political developments in J&K state had radical impact on the practices, rituals, values and norms of marriage, especially related directly to late marriage. Second, more important, politically oriented developments in last 20 years of militancy had further changing impact on the traditional pattern of late marriage in Kashmir. As a result, a situation has been created in which emergence of late marriage seemed as an established fact of life. The sociological analysis of this crucial phenomenon through various dimensions and factors is the central theme of this survey.

2. Methodology:

This survey stands primarily as an empirical survey about the phenomenon of emergence of late marriage in the Kashmir valley. No pre-conceived theoretical or ideological framework was used to observe and explain the relevant phenomenon. Among other reasons, this was done to avoid any kind of bias in the findings of the survey. The universe of this survey was whole valley of Kashmir composing of ten following administrative districts:

Table 2.1. Details about the Universe of Survey undertaken

S. No.	*District*	*No. of Respondents*	*S. No.*	*District*	*No. of Respondents*
1.	Srinagar	225	2.	Anantnag	150
3.	Baramulla	125	4.	Kupwara	100
5.	Bandipora	100	6.	Pulwama	150
7.	Shopian	150	8.	Ganderbal	150
9.	Kulgam	150	10.	Budgam	200

The methods and techniques of data collection in this survey were questionnaire and interview. A detailed questionnaire was formulated for the purpose of collecting primary source information from respondents. It composed of questions on important selected themes. It had stratified, open-ended and fixed-choice questions, which were filled by trained investigators in the presence of respondents or in absentia. The responses were recorded cautiously in order to maintain originality and specificity of responses.

The sample in this survey was highly intensive and stratified in order to include more groups and communities. It was also highly representative to all relevant collectivities of respondents. The sociological variables became the basis for selection of respondents. These specific variables were identified as sex, age, literacy, income, marital-status and rural-urban status. The total number of respondents in the sample was 1,500 who composed the categories shown in following tables:

Table 2.2. Composition of Age Groups of the Sample

S. No.	*Respondent's*	*Age Groups [No.]*		*Total*		
	Cluster No.	*00-25 yrs.*	*26-40 yrs.*	*41+ yrs.*	*No.*	*percentage*
1.	01-50	18	14	18	50	03.33
2.	51-100	13	25	12	50	03.33
3.	101-150	13	25	12	50	03.33
4.	151-200	12	25	13	50	03.33
5.	201-250	13	25	12	50	03.33
6.	251-300	16	23	11	50	03.33
7.	301-350	18	14	18	50	03.33
8.	351-400	13	25	12	50	03.33
9.	401-450	13	25	12	50	03.33
10.	451-500	06	44	04	50	03.33
11.	501-550	13	25	12	50	03.33
12.	551-600	12	24	14	50	03.33
13.	601-650	13	25	12	50	03.33
14.	651-700	15	20	15	50	03.33
15.	701-750	20	15	15	50	03.33
16.	751-800	13	25	12	50	03.33
17.	801-850	13	25	12	50	03.33
18.	851-900	20	16	14	50	03.33
19.	901-950	17	23	10	50	03.33
20.	951-1000	13	25	12	50	03.33
21.	1001-1050	13	25	12	50	03.33
22.	1051-1100	13	25	12	50	03.33
23.	1101-1150	12	24	14	50	03.33
24.	1151-1200	25	15	10	50	03.33
25.	1201-1250	17	17	16	50	03.33
26.	1251-1300	13	25	12	50	03.33
27.	1301-1350	16	24	12	50	03.33

28.	1351-1400	17	15	18	50	03.33
29.	1401-1450	14	26	10	50	03.33
30.	1451-1500	18	14	18	50	03.33
	Total	442	678	370	1500	100.00
		29.40	45.20	24.60	100.00	

Table 2.3. Composition of Income Groups of the Sample

S.No.	*Respondent's Cluster No.*	*Upto 10000*	*10000 - 25000*	*25001+*	*Total No.*	*percentage*
1.	01-50	14	22	14	50	03.33
2.	51-100	23	20	07	50	03.33
3.	101-150	15	22	13	50	03.33
4.	151-200	16	22	12	50	03.33
5.	201-250	15	25	10	50	03.33
6.	251-300	44	05	01	50	03.33
7.	301-350	14	22	14	50	03.33
8.	350-400	23	20	07	50	03.33
9.	401-450	23	20	07	50	03.33
10.	451-500	39	07	04	50	03.33
11.	501-550	13	25	12	50	03.33
12.	551-600	10	20	20	50	03.33
13.	601-650	18	20	12	50	03.33
14.	651-700	15	20	15	50	03.33
15.	701-750	20	15	15	50	03.33
16.	751-800	24	10	16	50	03.33
17.	801-850	20	15	15	50	03.33
18.	851-900	20	15	15	50	03.33
19.	901-950	18	26	06	50	03.33
20.	951-1000	27	13	10	50	03.33
21.	1001-1050	15	25	10	50	03.33
22.	1051-1100	21	26	03	50	03.33

23.	1101-1150	24	16	19	50	03.33
24.	1151-1200	17	18	15	50	03.33
25.	1201-1250	25	15	10	50	03.33
26.	1251-1300	20	15	15	50	03.33
27.	1301-1350	25	13	12	50	03.33
28.	1351-1400	15	25	10	50	03.33
29.	1401-1450	25	15	10	50	03.33
30.	1451-1500	16	24	10	50	03.33
	Total	614	557	329	1500	100.00
			40.90%	37.10%	21.90%	100.00

Table 2.4. Composition of Sex Groups of the Sample

S. No.	*Respondents Cluster No.*	*Male*	*Female*	*Total No.*	*percentage*
1.	01-50	26	24	50	03.33
2.	51-100	25	25	50	03.33
3.	101-150	25	25	50	03.33
4.	151-200	25	25	50	03.33
5.	201-250	25	25	50	03.33
6.	251-300	29	21	50	03.33
7.	301-350	26	24	50	03.33
8.	351-400	25	25	50	03.33
9.	401-450	25	25	50	03.33
10.	451-500	25	25	50	03.33
11.	501-550	25	25	50	03.33
12.	551-600	25	25	50	03.33
13.	601-650	26	24	50	03.33
14.	651-700	28	22	50	03.33
15.	701-750	30	20	50	03.33
16.	750-800	26	24	50	03.33
17.	801-850	25	25	50	03.33

18.	851-900	25	25	50	03.33
19.	901-950	31	19	50	03.33
20.	951-1000	25	25	50	03.33
21.	1001-1050	25	25	50	03.33
22.	1051-1100	25	25	50	03.33
23.	1101-1150	26	24	50	03.33
24.	1151-1200	29	21	50	03.33
25.	1201-1250	25	25	50	03.33
26.	1251-1300	25	25	50	03.33
27.	1301-1350	25	25	50	03.33
28.	1351-1400	26	24	50	03.33
29.	1401-1450	28	22	50	03.33
30.	1451-1500	26	24	50	03.33
	Total	782	718	1500	100.00
		52.13%	47.80%	100.00%	

Table 2.5. Marital Status of the Respondents of the Sample

S.No.	*Respondents Cluster no.*	*Married*	*Unmarried*	*Total No.*	*percentage*
1.	01-50	30	20	50	03.33
2.	51-100	31	19	50	03.33
3.	101-150	26	24	50	03.33
4.	151-200	24	26	50	03.33
5.	201-250	28	22	50	03.33
6.	251-300	32	18	50	03.33
7.	301-350	30	20	50	03.33
8.	351-400	31	19	50	03,33
9.	401-450	31	19	50	03.33
10.	451-500	30	20	50	03.33
11.	501-550	36	14	50	03.33
12.	551-600	34	16	50	03.33

13.	601-650	26	24	50	03.33
14.	651-700	25	25	50	03.33
15.	701-750	26	24	50	03.33
16.	751-800	25	25	50	03.33
17.	801-850	25	25	50	03.33
18.	851-900	26	24	50	03.33
19.	901-950	31	19	50	03.33
20.	951-1000	27	23	50	03.33
21.	1001-1050	28	22	50	03.33
22.	1051-1100	32	18	50	03.33
23.	1101-1150	28	22	50	03.33
24.	1151-1200	27	23	50	03.33
25.	1201-1250	26	24	50	03.33
26.	1251-1300	33	17	50	03.33
27.	1301-1350	30	20	50	03.33
28.	1351-1400	31	19	50	03.33
29.	1401-1450	27	23	50	03.33
30.	1451-1500	19	31	50	03.33
	Total	855	645	1500	100.00
		57.00%	43.00%	100.00%	

Table 2.6. Literacy Status of Respondents of the Sample

S.No.	*Respondents Cluster No.*	*Literate*	*Illiterate*	*Total No.*	*percentage*
1.	01-50	32	18	50	03.33
2.	51-100	36	14	50	03.33
3.	101-150	32	18	50	03.33
4.	151-200	30	20	50	03.33
5.	201-250	34	16	50	03.33
6.	251-300	34	16	50	03.33
7.	301-350	32	18	50	03.33
8.	351-400	36	14	50	03.33
9.	401-450	36	14	50	03.33

10.	451-500	30	20	50	03.33
11.	501-550	36	14	50	03.33
12.	551-600	30	20	50	03.33
13.	601-650	24	26	50	03.33
14.	651-700	30	20	50	03.33
15.	701-750	29	21	50	03.33
16.	751-800	30	20	50	03.33
17.	801-850	26	24	50	03.33
18.	851-900	24	26	50	03.33
19.	901-950	37	13	50	03.33
20.	951-1000	41	09	50	03.33
21.	1001-1050	34	16	50	03.33
22.	1051-1100	41	09	50	03.33
23.	1101-1150	34	16	50	03.33
24.	1151-1200	44	06	50	03.33
25.	1201-1250	35	15	50	03.33
26.	1251-1300	25	25	50	03.33
27.	1301-1350	25	25	50	03.33
28.	1351-1400	30	20	50	03.33
29.	1401-1450	26	24	50	03.33
30.	1451-1500	20	30	50	03.33
	Total	951	549	1500	100.00
		63.40%	36.60%	100.00%	

Table 2. 7. Rural/Urban Status of Respondents of the Sample

S. No.	*Respondents Cluster No.*	*Rural Area No.*	*Urban Area No.*	*Total No.*	*percentage*
1.	01-503	4	16	50	03.33
2.	51-100	44	06	50	03.33
3.	101-150	30	20	50	03.33
4.	151-200	30	20	50	03.33
5.	201-250	14	36	50	03.33
6.	251-300	39	11	50	03.33
7.	301-350	34	16	50	03.33

8.	351-400	44	06	50	03.33
9.	401-450	44	06	50	03.33
10.	451-500	40	10	50	03.33
11.	501-550	43	07	50	03.33
12.	551-600	40	10	50	03.33
13.	601-650	30	20	50	03.33
14.	651-700	15	35	50	03.33
15.	701-750	17	33	50	03.33
16.	750-800	44	06	50	03.33
17.	801-850	35	15	50	03.33
18.	851-900	31	19	50	03.33
19.	901-950	33	17	50	03.33
20.	951-1000	26	24	50	03.33
21.	1001-1050	14	36	50	03.33
22.	1051-1100	25	25	50	03.33
23.	1101-1150	40	10	50	03.33
24.	1151-1200	37	13	50	03.33
25.	1201-1250	37	13	50	03.33
26.	1251-1300	30	20	50	03.33
27.	1301-1350	35	15	50	03.33
28.	1351-1400	30	20	50	03.33
29.	1401-1450	38	12	50	03.33
30.	1451-1500	34	16	50	03.33
	Total	987	513	1500	100.00
		65 %	34.20 %	100.00 %	

After formulation of the questionnaire, the investigators were trained in detail about filling in the field, so that originality and specificity of responses was recorded properly and completely. The trained investigators of this survey were 30 M.A. final students of Department of Sociology of University of Kashmir. In fact, they had opted for this course for which they were guided, supervised, evaluated and graded.

The detailed fieldwork for this survey was carried out for a period of five months from June 2007 to October 2007 as per the 'field action plan'. According to this plan, the entire research for this survey among all 1500 respondents of the sample was carried out in 30 equal clusters of respondents. While each cluster composed of 50 respondents, each investigator surveyed 50 respondents. In totality, 30 investigators carried out scientific investigation among 1500 respondents who belonged to varied sociological categories. As they were trained in advance, researchers selected these particular groups of respondents on the basis of sociological criteria of age, sex, income, literacy, marital status and rural/urban status. In this way, the sample of respondents was made reflective, realistic, relevant and representative.

After statistical data was collected in the field, it was aggregated and tabulated at the cluster average and total average levels. The tables were made on the basis of main themes of the survey. Subsequently, these tables were explained, interpreted and conclusions drawn scientifically and sociologically.

3. Findings of The Survey

3.1.1. Average Age /Desirable Age of Marriage: Every society decides about a particular age at which its young members are supposed to marry. In a way, it may be characterised as 'desirable age of marriage' for men and women. But due to certain factors, marriage of men and women do not take place at desirable age but occurs at a later stage which may be characterised as 'actual age of marriage'. In this context, we enquired from respondents about actual and desirable age of marriage for men as well as women. The response they showed has been included in the following table:

Table 3.1. Actual and Desirable Age of Marriage

S.No.	*Respondents*	*Actual Age of Marriage*		*Desirable Age of Marriage*	
	Cluster No.	*Males*	*Females*	*Males*	*Females*
1.	01-50	32	28	22	19
2.	51-100	23	21	18	16
3.	101-150	33	29	25	23
4.	151-200	29	25	23	21
5.	201-250	34	31	25	22

6.	251-300	32	27	25	21
7.	301-350	33	26	24	21
8.	351-400	30	28	22	20
9.	401-450	23	21	18	16
10.	451-500	32	28	25	21
11.	501-550	31	29	24	21
12.	551-600	33	29	25	23
13.	601-650	35	31	25	22
14.	651-700	36	30	24	20
15.	701-750	39	29	24	21
16.	751-800	30	28	22	20
17.	801-850	32	28	26	22
18.	851-900	37	31	28	24
19.	901-950	31	28	23	20
20.	951-1000	30	26	24	21
21.	1001-1050	34	31	24	21
22.	1051-1100	27	25	25	19
23.	1101-1150	34	31	24	21
24.	1151-1200	31	27	23	20
25.	1201-1250	32	28	24	22
26.	1251-1300	33	31	22	19
27.	1301-1350	35	30	24	22
28.	1351-1400	26	24	24	21
29.	1401-1450	34	30	23	18
30.	1451-1500	30	26	24	21
	Total no. of responses	946	835	709	621
	Average age of marriage	31.53	27.83	23.63	20.70

The above details clearly show the following 'age of marriage' for males and females on a average;

[i]	Actual age of marriage	Males	31.53 years
		Females	27.83 years
[ii]	Desirable age of marriage	Males	23.63 years
		Females	20.70 years

3.2 *Major Causes of Late Marriage:* The survey revealed that there were five major factors which led to emergence of late marriage in the Kashmir valley. These factors were

[i]	Acute poverty	865/1500	[57.66 per cent] respondents
[ii]	Increasing unemployment	840/1500	[56.00 per cent] respondents
[iii]	Dowry in different shapes	840/1500	[56.00 per cent] respondents
[iv]	Attain. Modern education	470/1500	[31.33 per cent] respondents
[v]	Present conflict situation	243/1500	[15.60 per cent] respondents

Other minor factors which contributed to the emergence of late marriage in Kashmir included the following factors:

[i]	Illiteracy	98/1500	[06.53 per cent] respondents
[ii]	Modernisation impact	98/1500	[06.53 per cent] respondents
[iii]	Health abnormality	71/1500	[04.73 per cent] respondents
[iv]	Customs and traditions	65/1500	[04.33 per cent] respondents
[v]	Caste consideration	64/1500	[04.26 per cent] respondents
[vi]	search for proper match	55/1500	[03.66 per cent] respondents

[vii] irreligious attitudes and behaviour 46/1500 [03.06 per cent] respondents

[viii] preference for employed woman 25/1500 [01.66 per cent] respondents

[ix] developing professional career 24/1500 [01.66 per cent] respondents

[x] love affairs/illegal sex relations 23/1500 [01.53 per cent] respondents

[xi] huge marriage expenditure 23/1500 [01.53 per cent] respondents

[xii] generation gap 22/1500 [01.46 per cent] respondents

[xiii] ignorance-innocence 18/1500 [01.20 per cent] respondents

[xiv] inflation in the market 15/1500 [01.00 per cent] respondents

3.2. *Consequences of Late Marriage:* The survey made an investigation about short-term and long-term implications of the late marriage phenomenon on the individuals and society at large. The respondents identified the following impacts:

[i] Decrease in population 365/1500 [24.33 per cent] respondents

[ii] various forms of mental depression 361/1500 [24.06 per cent] respondents

[iii] increase in suicide rate 295/1500 [19.66 per cent] respondents

[iv] encouragement to immoral activities 182/1500 [12.13 per cent] respondents

[v] pre-marital sex relations 157/1500 [10.46 per cent] respondents

The respondents also identified the following minor consequences of the emergence of late marriage in Kashmir:

[i]	abnormal child birth	148/1500	[09.86 per cent] respondents
[ii]	lack of child care	143/1500	[09.53 per cent] respondents
[iii]	increase in crimes/social deviance	137/1500	[09.13 per cent] respondents
[iv]	frustration of the youth	90/1500	[06.00 per cent] respondents
[v]	disturbed social-family life	67/1500	[04.46 per cent] respondents
[vi]	Age gap between parents and children	59/1500	[03.93 per cent] respondents
[vii]	sex scandals	47/1500	[03.13 per cent] respondents
[viii]	Tension among the youth	44/1500	[02.93 per cent] respondents
[ix]	increase in divorces	41/1500	[02.73 per cent] respondents
[x]	family problems-instability	38/1500	[02.53 per cent] respondents
[xi]	girls remained unmarried	37/1500	[02.46 per cent] respondents
[xii]	imbalanced sex ratio	26/1500	[01.73 per cent] respondents
[xiii]	drug addiction	22/1500	[01.46 per cent] respondents
[xiv]	alienation	18/1500	[01.20 per cent] respondents

3.3. *Modern Education and Late Marriage:* There is general belief that attainment of modern education especially at higher level and in technical-professional fields takes a long time. So, men and women involved in this process usually experienced late marriage in their lives. This basic proposition was confirmed in this survey as about 85.00 per cent respondents agreed when they were asked to explain this response. They gave responses in following ways:

[i]	modern education is time-taking	875/1500	[58.33 per cent] respondents
[ii]	educated people wait for proper job	203/1500	[13.53 per cent] respondents
[iii]	educated people face competition of jobs	83/1500	[05.53 per cent] respondents
[iv]	educated people search for equal educated Partner	60/1500	[04.00 per cent] respondents
[v]	educated people desire for employed spouse	48/1500	[03.20 per cent] respondents
[vi]	educated people deviate from tradition and religion	27/1500	[01.80 per cent] respondents
[vii]	rational thinking compels them for one marriage	25/1500	[01.65 per cent] respondents

However, about 15.00 per cent respondents revealed that attainment of modern education does not contribute directly to emergence of late marriage. Though this seems a correct statement, modern education does not contribute solely to this phenomenon. This response reflects essentially the emphasis on the role of other contributing factors such as poverty, unemployment and other personal problems.

3.4. *Poverty and Late Marriage:* The general belief in Kashmir is that poverty in all possibilities leads to the emergence of late marriage among poor sections of society. In this survey, about 88.00 per cent of respondents upheld that when poor people are not in a position to pay for necessary expenses of marriage, it automatically gets delayed. When we asked them to provide the rationale for this argument, the made the statements which follow:

[i]	Poor girls can never pay dowry	566/1500	[37.73 per cent] respondents
[ii]	Lack of financial resources for marriage	388/1500	[25.86 per cent] respondents
[iii]	Lot of expenditure on marriage ceremony	305/1500	[20.33 per cent] respondents
[iv]	Poor girls are not preferred in marriages at all	155/1500	[10.33 per cent] respondents
[v]	illiteracy of girls	61/1500	[04.06 per cent] respondents
[vi]	non-fulfillment of demands by girls family	59/1500	[03.93 per cent] respondents
[vii]	parents arrange money somehow	55/1500	[03.66 per cent] respondents
[viii]	argument that poor girls cannot maintain family	35/1500	[02.33 per cent] respondents
[ix]	simple barrier to a good marriage	32/1500	[02.13 per cent] respondents

3.5. *Conflict Situation and Late Marriage;* As the fact stands, conflict situation in Kashmir had certainly contributed to the emergence of late marriage. An overwhelming majority of 88.00 per cent respondents in this survey gave this opinion. When they were asked to provide the rationale for this opinion, they conveyed the following views:

[i]	youth was involved/killed during conflict situation	274/1500	[14.13 per cent] respondents
[ii]	conflict created sex imbalance in marriage market	274/1500	[14.13 per cent] respondents
[iii]	death of the sole earning member of the family	200/1500	[13.33 per cent] respondents
[iv]	conflict created unemployment and poverty	169/1500	[11.26 per cent] respondents
[v]	threat and involvement in militancy	122/1500	[08.13 per cent] respondents
[vi]	avoidance of militancy related families	77/1500	[05.13 per cent] respondents
[vii]	migration to outside state for several reasons	61/1500	[04.06 per cent] respondents
[viii]	conflict created insecurity of life in the valley	48/1500	[03.20 per cent] respondents
[ix]	conflict often disturbed family functions	32/1500	[01.40 per cent] respondents

However, 12.00 per cent respondents in this survey opined that conflict situation was not directly responsible for the phenomenon of delayed marriage in Kashmir. This response essentially conveys two points. First, conflict situation was not the sole determining factor for delayed marriages in the valley. Second, there were other factors equally important in the broader social dynamics which played their respective roles in the emergence of late marriage in the Valley.

3.6. *Dowry and Late Marriage*: As is a known fact, dowry has played certain negative role towards normal marriage in Kashmir. It has created numerous problems for individuals and families. One such problem created by dowry was late marriage which could not be avoided in a situation in which dowry demands were made by the groom's side. These views were also conveyed by about 92.00 per cent of respondents. When they were asked to explain these views, they made the following points:

[i]	poor families can never afford to pay dowry	822/1500	[54.80 per cent] respondents
[ii]	Many males refuse to marry without getting dowry	106/1500	[07.06 per cent] respondents
[iii]	Dowry proved a barrier to early marriage	88/1500	[05.86 per cent] respondents
[iv]	girls feel inferior if they don't get dowry	86/1500	[05.73 per cent] respondents
[v]	unemployed girls could never pay even little dowry	48/1500	[03.20 per cent] respondents
[vi]	dowry has made marriage a commercial affair	42/1500	[02.80 per cent] respondents
[vii]	money-collection for dowry a time-consuming affair	37/1500	[02.46 per cent] respondents

[viii] Dowry as a customary practice
to be followed 36/1500 [02.40 per cent] respondents

[ix] non-payment of dowry
leads to suicides by girls 28/1500 [01.86 per cent] respondents

[x] difficult to find a 'good family'
not demanding dowry 26/1500 [01.73 per cent] respondents

[xi] harassment of girls in case
they don't pay any dowry 25/1500 [01.66 per cent] respondents

[xii] non-payment of dowry
leads to girls depression 24/1500 [01.65 per cent] respondents

[xiii] poor girls wait for long time
to get dowry-less marriage 23/1500 [01.53 per cent] respondents

[xiv] those who don't pay dowry are
often poor and illiterate 10/1500 [00.66 per cent] respondents

[xv] non-payment of dowry may
lead to divorce 10/1500 [00.66 per cent] respondents

3.7. *Unemployment and Late Marriage:* It has been generally established that increasing unemployment hassled to the emergence of late marriage in Kashmir. About 91.00 per cent of respondents upheld this kind of opinion. This situation could not be controlled in any way. In this regard, when the respondents were probed further, they presented the following views:

[i] unemployed boys and girls were
not considered good 408/1500 [27.20 per cent] respondents

[ii] unemployed prefer to get jobs and then marry 352/1500 [27.20 per cent] respondents

[iii] unemployed cannot take responsibility of the family 141/1500 [09.40 per cent] respondents

[iv] unemployed girls cannot pay dowry to boy's family 128/1500 [08.53 per cent] respondents

[v] unemployed cannot bear the expenditure of marriage 89/1500 [05.93 per cent] respondents

[vi] unemployed youth often remain disturbed 45/1500 [03.00per cent] respondents

[vii] unemployed maintain poor economic status 40/1500 [02.66 per cent] respondents

[viii] unemployment creates insecurity among boys and girls 23/1500 [01.53 per cent] respondents

However, 09.00 per cent respondents presented the view that unemployment does not contribute directly to the rise of late marriage. In reality, they wanted to emphasie the role of other important factors responsible for emergence of late marriage.

3.8. *Pre-marital Sex and Late Marriage:* The survey revealed an inverse relationship between late marriage and practices of pre-marital and extra-marital relations among the most potent section of society, i.e., youth. In response to our question regarding consequences of late marriage on existing sex relations, 64.46 per cent [976 out of 1500] respondents conveyed that it effected the pre-marital relations in particular. They cited following reasons in order to provide the rationale for their response:

[i] Since sex is a biological need, the youths want to satisfy the sexual needs 768/1500 [51.20 per cent] respondents

[ii] The sex control is not possible at all times, since it is at its peak at the younger age. 182.1500 [12.13 per cent] respondents

[iii] There is clear deviation from religious values and there is lack of mora knowledge. 29/1500 [01.93 per cent] respondents.

At the same time, 219/1500 [14.60 per cent] respondents conveyed that the increasing practice of late marriage has led to extra-marital relationship, especially among elder and married sections of society. They quoted more or less same reasons as referred in the preceding case.

3.9. *Local Culture and Late Marriage:* Every culture necessarily influences the patterns of marriage. So is the case with Kashmiri society. In response to our question 'whether local culture has influenced late marriage in Kashmir', 840/1500 [56.00 per cent] respondents conveyed 'yes' in their reply. The reasons they put forward were as follows:

[i] people generally imitate the practice of late marriage without considering its consequences. 413/1500 [27.53 per cent] respondents

[ii] the traditional 'wazwan' has become unaffordable for many people. 110/1500 [07.33 per cent] respondents

[iii] unnecessary customs and rituals which discourage early/timely marriage 185/1500 [12/.33 per cent] respondents

[iv] common demand of dowry by boy's family which necessarily leads to late marriage 168/1500 [11.20 per cent] respondents

[v] Changing culture fails to determine timely marriage 84/1500 [05.60 per cent] respondents

[vi] Rich people encourage late marriage and encourage others to follow this practice. 44/1500 [02.93 per cent] respondents

On the other hand, 326/1500 [21.37 per cent] respondents gave the opinion that local culture has not in any way encouraged late marriage. They gave following reasons for their response:

[i] Our culture demands early-timely marriage, especially of girls. 108/1500 [07.20 per cent] respondents

[ii] Since culture and religion are interrelated, they cannot favour emergence of late marriage. 89/1500 [05.93 per cent] respondents

[iii] Culture has nothing to do with late marriage 44/1500 [02.93 per cent] respondents

[iv] Culture discourages late marriage. 21/1500 [01.40 per cent] respondents

[v] It happens mainly due to false prestige. 14/1500 [00.93 per cent] respondents

3.10. *Late Marriage and Role of Religion:* In this empirical survey, the important question about role of religion vis-à-vis late marriage was asked from the respondents. The dominant response to this question was conveyed that religion has not encouraged late marriage among its followeRs It has rather discouraged it for latent and manifest reasons. When we probed among respondents as how religion discouraged late marriage, 1059/1500 [70.60 per cent] respondents said that it [religion] emphasised early marriage in all possibilities and in all situations. Further, 45/1500 [03.00 per cent] respondents opined that religion discouraged late marriage because the early marriage stops individual and society from many social evils. These responses were recorded despite the fact that late marriage has emerged as a significant type of marriage in the present-day Kashmiri society. It follows that religion is not followed strictly in this society.

On the other hand, only 53/1500 [03.53 per cent] repondents said that religion encouraged late marriage. But, they had given neither theoretical nor practical given justification in this regard.

3.11. *Late Marriage and Marriage Practices:* It has been observed in this survey that emergence of late marriage in Kashmir has certainly effected the existing patters and practices of marriage. It was recorded that while hyper-gamy was effected in the case of 571/1500 [38.06 per cent] respondents, late marriage had also effected in 132/1500 [08.80 per cent] hypo-gamous cases . Again, 442/1500 [29.46 per cent] respondents reported the influence of late marriage on endogamy and by 137/1500 [09.13 per cent] respondents on the exogamous marriages. While 280/1500 [18.66 per cent] respondents conveyed the influence on polygamous marriages, 129/1500 [08.60 per cent] on monogamous marriages. Lastly, late marriage had influenced considerably the practices related to patri-locality and matri-locality.

3.12. *Problems of Late Marriage:* In the social dynamics related to emergence of late marriage, several problems cropped up and created serious difficulties for concerned individuals and families. In the survey, they reported the following problems:

[i]	mental depression and other psychological problems	363/1500	[24.20 per cent] respondents
[ii]	population decrease and infertility at large	308/1500	[20.53 per cent] respondents
[iii]	pre-marital sex relations	240/1500	[16.00 per cent] respondents
[iv]	increase in suicide rate	170/1500	[11.33 per cent] respondents

[v]	late child birth with associated problems	161/1500	[10.73 per cent] respondents
[vi]	increase in immoral and vulgar activities	124/1500	[08.26 per cent] respondents
[vii]	post-marital discord in the family	111/1500	[07.40 per cent] respondents
[viii]	Rise of particular diseases among children and elders	91/1500	[06.60 per cent] respondents
[ix]	generation gap widened within family	91/1500	[06.60 per cent] respondents
[x]	Increase in crimes and divorces	89/1500	[05.93 per cent] respondents
[xi]	increase in drug addiction	88/1500	[05.86 per cent] respondents
[xii]	sex scandals and social disorders	70/1500	[04.66 per cent] respondents
[xiii]	lesser child care in the parental family	56/1500	[03.73 per cent] respondents
[xiv]	cronic family tensions	40/1500	[02.66 per cent] respondents
[xv]	health problems of the couple	24/1500	[01.60 per cent] respondents
[xvi]	rise in materialistic views	12/1500	[00.80 per cent] respondents

3.13. *Modernisation and Late Marriage:* The emergence of late marriage had direct relationship with the process of modernisation. In fact, there seemed necessary social impact of modernisation on marriage practices as happened in Kashmiri society too. In our enquiry about late marriage and modernisation, we recorded the following responses:

[i]	modernisation emphasised higher education	298/1500	[19.86 per cent] respondents
[ii]	modernisation cautioned about ill effects of marriage	103/1500	[06.86 per cent] respondents
[iii]	modernisation gave human life the materialistic outlook	97/1500	[06.46 per cent] respondents
[iv]	modernisation changed traditional ideals of marriage	94/1500	[06.26 per cent] respondents
[v]	modernisation encouraged late marriage	73/1500	[04.86 per cent] respondents
[vi]	modernisation followed new fashions of life	71/1500	[04.73 per cent] respondents
[vii]	modernisation led to deviation from religion	64/1500	[04.26 per cent] respondents
[viii]	modernisation created competitive and complex life	62/1500	[04.13 per cent] respondents
[ix]	modernisation gave career orientation	47/1500	[03.13 per cent] respondents

[x] modernisation created lust for money 46/1500 [03.06 per cent] respondents

[xi] it took long time for career-making of the life-mate 43/1500 [02,86 per cent] respondents

[xii] usually men want highly qualified wife 26/1500 [01.73 per cent] respondents

[xiii] modernisation encouraged pre-marital sex relationship 20/1500 [01.33 per cent] respondents

[xiv] self-choice marriage goes up and up 11/1500 [00.73 per cent] respondents

[xv] media impact encouraged late marriage 10/1500 [00.66 per cent] respondents

3.14. *Self -choice Marriage and Late Marriage:* It was observed in the survey that self-choice marriage does and does not lead to late marriage. In the former case, 625/1500 [41.66 per cent] respondents maintained that self-choice marriage necessarily led to late marriage. The reasons they cited included their self-choice to marry at a particular time [31.86 per cent], wait for a suitable match [10.33 per cent] and attainment of education and employment [01.73 per cent] .

On the other hand, 456/1500 [30.40 per cent] respondents conveyed their opinion that self-choice marriage does not necessarily led to late marriage for the following reasons:

[i] lovers choice generally led to early marriage 234/1500 [15.60 per cent] respondents

[ii] self-choice marriage stood for a time-bound marriage 44/1500 [02.93 per cent] respondents

[iii] Self-choice mates hardly took care for customs 32/1500 [02.13 per cent] respondents

[iv] mates don't faced the problem of dowry 23/1500 [01.53 per cent] respondents

3.15. *Suggestions about Late Marriage:* In continuation of the topic of problems of late marriage, the respondents in this survey stressed for the consideration of serious and relevant suggestions. Some of these are noted below:

[i] there must be legal restrictions or complete ban on dowry 374/1500 [24.93 per cent] respondents

[ii] parents must arrange timely marriages of children 275/1500 [18.40 per cent] respondents

[iii] children must follow religion seriously and strictly 265/1500 [17.66 per cent] respondents

[iv] employment must be provided to marriageable youth 207/1500 [13.80 per cent] respondents

[v] marriages must be made less expensive and affordable 94/1500 [06.26 per cent] respondents

[vi] awareness campaign against ill effects of late marriage 87/1500 [05.80 per cent] respondents

[vii] undesirable customs abolished and guest control intro. 70/1500 [04.66 per cent] respondents

[viii] marriages made simple. 65/1500 [04.33 per cent] respondents

[ix]	religion must be followed in all marriage matters	48/1500	[03.20 per cent] respondents
[x]	education to females even after marriage	40/1500	[02.66 per cent] respondents
[xi]	necessary changes in customs, attitudes and behaviour	38/1500	[02.53 per cent] respondents
[xii]	poverty must be eradicated through all means	33/1500	[02.20 per cent] respondents
[xiii]	population education for the youth	64/1500	[04.26 per cent] respondents

4. **Conclusions:**

The following conclusions may be drawn from preceding findings of the survey:

[a] The practice of late marriage has been established in the Kashmir society. The actual and desirable age of marriage was as follows;

Actual age of marriage	males	31.53 years
	females	27.83 years
Desirable age of marriage	males	23.63 years
	females	20.70 years

[b] The five major causes of late marriage in Kashmir identified by respondents were

- acute poverty
- increasing unemployment
- practice of dowry
- attainment of modern education
- prevailing conflict situation

[c] The five major consequences of late marriage were identified as follows:

- decrease in population at family level
- mental depression
- increase in suicide rate
- encouragement to immoral activities
- pre-marital sex relations

[d] 85 per cent respondents agreed with the proposition that attainment of modern education has led to the emergence of late marriage among males and females.

[e] 88 per cent respondents conveyed that poverty led to the emergence of late marriage, especially among poor groups and classes.

[f] 88 per cent respondents revealed their opinion that conflict situation in Kashmir had ontributed to the rise of late marriage.

[g] 92 per cent respondents upheld that emergence of late marriage could not be avoided in a situation in which dowry demands were made by the groom's family.

[h] 91 per cent respondents revealed that unemployment in all cases contributed to the rise of late marriage in Kashmir.

[i] 65 per cent respondents divulged the inverse relationship between late marriage and practices of pre-marital and extra-marital relations among the youth.

[j] While majority of 56 per cent respondents felt that local culture has influenced late marriage in Kashmir, the rest felt that it had discouraged the practice.

[k] the dominant number of respondents was of the opinion that religion, Islam, had not encouraged the late marriage, rather discouraged it for latent and manifest reasons.

[l] The late marriage effected in positive or negative way existing practices of hypergamy-hypogamy, polygamy-monogamy and patri-locality and matri-locality.

[m] Among important problems emerged due to late marriage included the following;

- mental depression, infertility, pre-marital sex relations, increase in suicide rate, late child birth, increasing immorality and vulgarity, post-marital family discord, diseases among children and elders, generation gap, increase in deviance and crime, drug addiction, social disorders, and lesser child care in family.

[n] The process of modernisation effected all practices of marriage, especially late marriage.

[o] The practice of self-choice marriage effected late marriage in 42 per cent cases and not in 31per cent cases.

[p] Finally, respondents put forth following suggestions for solving problems created by late marriage.

- complete ban or legal restriction on dowry,
- parents arrange their children's marriage at proper age,
- marriageable children follow religion seriously and strictly,
- employment must be provided to all marriageable youth,
- marriage must be made simple and affordable,
- creating awareness about ill effects of late marriage,
- undesirable customs must be rejected and abolished,
- education to women even after marriage,
- change in attitudes and behaviour,
- poverty eradicated through all means, and
- population education for youth.

17

Expanding Social Base of Crime in Kashmir

1. The fact stands with reasonable evidence that the traditional society in Kashmir was completely peaceful in attitudes and non-violent in behaviour. In this kind of social situation, there was very less scope for the existence of major or minor trends of crime, especially in an organised form and with institutional support. But, this situation was exposed to the forces, processes and implications of modernisation and development. In actuality, these macro-level forces initiated formally the processes of urbanisation, industrialisation, educational expansion, social-economic mobility, cultural exposure, demographic shifts and, particularly, adoption of materialistic ideology, attitudes and behaviour. With several broader social implications, these processes were associated with the social pathology in extreme form among most active groups, especially youngsteRs This emergence of pathological environment was glaringly clear from many social-psychological problems such as depression, tension, stress, anxiety, insecurity, suicidal tendency, threat perception, drug addiction alcoholism, social deviation and pervasive sex practices. All these problems created congenial conditions for incidence and occurrence of crime on the part of deviant groups. When the criminalisation of attitude and behaviour got ideational support, it was established and stabilised in the society and played havoc with ethical basis of social ethos.

2. This kind of crime situation emerged not only in J&K state but in the whole country. It reflects clearly in the annual reports collected and released by the National Crime Records Bureau [NCRB], Ministry of Home Affairs, New Delhi, regularly in previous decades. In its latest report in 2011, the NCBR revealed that:

   About 10,670 children were kidnapped or abducted in the last year;

   As many as 5,484 children were sexually assaulted in India in 2010;

1,408 others were killed in different parts of the country;

The age group of 18-30 years was the worst victim of violent crimes last year with 15,787 young people, including 4,207 females, losing their lives across the country;

A total of 13,134 people, including 3,957 females, belonging to the age group of 30-50 years, were killed in violent crimes last year, while 3,339 others of 50 plus years age group lost their lives in such crimes;

727 children, including 343 girls, in the age group of up to 10 years were also killed in violent crimes in the country;

The national capital, Delhi, has the highest number of kidnapping of children in the country, i.e., 2,962 in 2010 followed by Bihar [[1,359], U. P. [1,225], Maharastra [729], Rajasthan [706], A. P. [581] and Gujarat [565]. See NCRB Report, 2011.

3. Though this situation of crime in the Kashmiri society was increasing and intensifying slowly, this process got boost with initiation of militancy and subsequent militarisation. This situation was the result of two main factoRs First, use or misuse of the gun by deviant groups and sub-groups for selfish ends, economic in nature, and not for political-ideological ends. When some criminal elements misused gun, with the official support, for selfish ends like amassing wealth, the crime wave could not be controlled and so intensified to the alarming level. Second, use or misuse of gun by the security forces, especially during anti-insurgency operations, led to all sorts of crimes and human rights violations, which formalised the 'criminalisation of society'. In this way, the armed forces contributed directly to the situation of violent crime in the valley. It is believed here that these security forces were responsible for introducing mass rape in Kashmir. This process too gave rise to social pathology characterised with above-mentioned features. Thus it may be argued that both processes of militancy and militarisation provided the backdrop in which crimes were started in an organised way.

4. Now, it has been established the processes of modernisation and development on the one hand and militancy and militarisation on the other contributed towards creation, sustenance and continuity of various activities related to crime in Kashmir. While the former were non-violent in implications, the latter's impact proved violent. An environment of crime and violence was created whose negative impact could not be avoided by any individual or group. The local print media systematically

portrayed this wave of crimes and some newspapers introduced daily and weekly columns and pages for separate reporting the crimes in the valley. In general, the local press reported the following aspects and features of crime in Kashmir:

Inhuman, subhuman and brutal killings and murders on the part of various factors;

All cases of death, injury, disability and disappearance of local people;

Kashmir as the most militarised zone and so most dangerous area in the world, as was characterised by the U.S. State Department also;

All major cases of killing, torture, harassment, insecurity, denial of basic human rights and social-psychological problems of youth in Kashmir;

All major cases of crimes and violence against women, especially rape, murder, molestation, eve-teasing, domestic violence and so on;

All major-minor cases of theft, stealing, deceit, family and property disputes, matrimonial discords, adulteration, fake currency, deviance, alcoholism, drug addiction and blackmailing.

The trend of increasing crimes in Kashmir also revealed from the crime statistics issued by the J&K Police. According to a J&K Police report, the following number of crimes was registered in Srinagar district only from 1989 to 2010:

S.No.	*Year*	*Cases registered*		*Total*
		Normal	*Militancy-related*	
1.	1989	3479	264	3743
2.	1990	1327	1425	2752
3.	1991	1467	1331	2798
4.	1992	1507	1882	3389
5.	1993	1616	1381	2997
6.	1994	1536	1293	2829
7.	1995	2023	1180	3203
8.	1996	3127	1460	4587
9.	1997	3481	1159	4640
10.	1998	3406	711	4117
11.	1999	2895	693	3588
12.	2000	2752	506	3258
13.	2001	3303	477	3780
14.	2002	3382	418	3800
15.	2003	3861	264	4125
16.	2004	3332	236	3568

17.	2005	3311	254	3565
18.	2006	3018	237	3255
19.	2007	2992	113	3105
20.	2008	2858	81	2939
21.	2009	3321	80	3401
22.	2010	2817	63	2880

The table reveals that higher number of crimes were committed and registered in urban-dominated district of Srinagar. More or less same crime situation prevailed in other towns of the valley. The yearly, monthly, weekly and daily occurrence rate of these crimes was as follows:

S.No.	*Year*	*yearly*	*monthly*	*weekly*	*daily*
1.	1989	3743	312	78	03
2.	1997	4650	388	97	03
3.	2010	2880	238	60	02

The above figures show clearly that comparatively higher rates of the occurrence of crime prevailed in previous decades in Kashmir. The causation of this situation has been explained earlier.

5. Now, it can be argued with theoretical and empirical support that crime situation was relatively static in Kashmir in pre-1947 period. But, minor crimes started in the post-1947 era mainly due to the social pathology associated with modernisation and development implications. This lower level of crime got boost after 1989 when twin processes of militancy and militarisation started their impact that directly led to violent crimes which involved murder, rape, disappearance, torture, injury and so on. Moreover, such a situation provided much needed institutional basis and legitimising support to all acts of crime. In other words, the crime scene got violent, organised, vulgarised and nationalistic dimensions partly with the social support from some deviant groups and sub-groups and partly with the support of armed forces and the government. In this way, a new situation of crime was created in Kashmir consciously which hurt every individual and group in society. In reality, this situation seems worst and alarming mainly due to the apathetic attitude of the government and its crime control agencies. In order to control and eliminate the crime from the society, there is the need of proper assessment of the problem in perspective, effective-purposeful-contextual measures, grand societal initiatives at ideational and practical level and finally effective role of crime control agencies.

18

Conclusion

[i] The explanation of trends of migration and patterns of population change in J&K in last chapters have sufficiently established the reciprocal relationship between these two demographic phenomena. It has also established the following propositions:

[a] Migration trends and population changes in J&K in the last six decades are inversely related and have developed mutual implications;

[b] Both these processes contributed to other set of processes of demographic transformation in the J&K state; and

[c] The basic demographic changes provided basis, help, initiative and necessitated to various processes of social transformation.

These three sociological propositions may lead to the scientific understanding of the existing demographic realities in the post-1947 era.

Relationship between migration trends and population changes

[ii] The identification and explanation of migration trends in J&K, especially in the Kashmir province [the focused area of this study] have certainly and positively contributed to various other processes of demographic character. While the out-migration has had positive as well as negative implications [from the point of view of locals], the in-migration has contributed to more negative than positive implications. It is generally felt here that migration trends in modern times, particularly after 1947, proved helpful to all classes, groups and communities in broader processes of change and development. While majority of businessmen-skilled-semiskilled labour migration has elevated many sections of society in terms of elevated economic status. Since the handicraft in Kashmir economy stands labour intensive and labouroriented, this economic

benefit was shared by many other lower and middle class segments. Morever, the annual official and unofficial migration during the harsh winter season to outside Kashmir to national and international destinations created a lot of chances for their economic mobility, which was necessarily associated with social mobility. The darbar-move migration contributed towards social, cultural, economic and other mobility. Thus all trends of migration, except the KP migration in 1990-1991, played a role in the change, progress and development.

[iii] However, negative implications were observed by the locals in two trends of migration. First, the KP migration in 1990-1991 uprooted the community from roots and it has not been able to return to it home due to various problems created during last 23 years Moreover, this mass migration of KPs snatched the multi-religious, composite culture and tradition of tolerance in Kashmir. Second, the labour migration in Kashmir, especially from Bihar, has contributed negatively giving rise to public sentiments against them. This labour migration not only replaced the local traditional labour in different fields, it has also led to increase of unemployment in the state. It has also contributed to the hostile environment between locals and migrants and establishment of slums, wherefrom drugs are manufactured and supplied to the local youth. Moreover, the illegal sexual activities are also carried out from these settlements.

[iv] Side by side with these migration trends, patterns of population change were also experienced in J&K consistently. While total population and its proportion increased at some levels and areas, it got reduced in other areas and at other levels. Again composition of all social collectivities got changed during last few decades. Some salient features of these changes in population in J&K state reflect in the following statistics:

Total population in the state: [in lakhs]

			Percentage		
Year	*Total*	*Males*	*Females*	*Rural*	*Urban*
1941	29.46	53.51	46.49	86.88	13.12
1951	32.54 [est.]	53.36	46.64	85.95	14.85
1961	35.68	53.25	46.75	83.34	16.66
1971	46.16	53.25	46.76	81.41	18.89

1981	59.89	52.84	47.16	78.95	21.83
1991	77.18 [est.]	52.00	48.00	76.79	23.83
2001	10.06 [mil.]	05.30 [mil.]	04.70 [mil.]		
2011	12548926	72.80	27.20		

Thus we get a total picture of the demographic transformation in the J&K state during the last eight decades from the above quoted statistics from census of J&K.

[v] Now after the presentation of basic facts and figures about trends of migration and patterns of migration changes, we are in a position to argue that these processes directly and indirectly contribute to wider processes of social transformation consistently and systematically and effected the social life in its entirety. This dynamics related to the migration trends and population changes on the one hand and these dynamics related to these processes and their impact on the initiation and concretisation of demographic transformation on the other leads us to a broader conclusion. That conclusion is that all these micro and macro level aspects/features of demographic transformation provides the matetial basis for the grand process of social transformation in the society. So, the entire dynamics concludes in social transition which in itself effects the dynamics of demographic realities for improvement and betterment of human society. This crucial relationship and dynamics of migration trends, population changes, demographic changes and finally social transformation is portrayed in the following diagram:

Relationship between Migration Trends, Population changes, Demographic Changes and Social Transformation.

[vi] Thus the above dynamics shown in the diagram explains the nature of relationship between migration trends, population changes, demographic changes and social transformation shows the related developments in the state of J&K in the last eight decades.

Bibliography

Bala, R., Trends in Urbanisation in India, Jaipur, 1986, Rawat Publishers.

Bhattacharya, A., Population Geography of India, New Delhi, 1978, Shree Publication House.

P. G. and Shasytri, A., Population in India: A Study of Inter-state Variation, New Delhi, 1976, Vikas Publishing House.

Bhuttani, Smitha, Demographic Dynamics in India, New Delhi, 1995, Discovery Press.

Bose, Ashish, Patterns of Population Change in India: 1951-1961, Bombay, 1967, Allied Press.

Census of India, 1951

1961

1971

1981

1991

2001 and

2011, Government of India, New Delhi.

Census of Jammu and Kashmir, 1961

1971

1981

1991

2001, and

2011, Government of J&K, Srinagar/Jammu.

Chandraman, R.C., A Geography of Population, New Delhi, 1986, Kalyani Publications.

Bibliography

Index

N

O

P